DATE DUE

OCT 2 6 2005		
DEC 1 0 2005		

DEMCO 38-296

SCIENCE FAIR PROJECTS

CHEMISTRY

Bob Bonnet & Dan Keen
Illustrated by Frances Zweifel

Sterling Publishing Co., Inc.
New York

This book is dedicated to
Bob's granddaughter Kaitlyn Louise Bonnet,
and Dan's granddaughter Anne Lynn Bodine.

Edited by Claire Bazinet

Library of Congress Cataloging-in-Publication Data Available

10 9 8 7 6 5 4 3 2 1

Published by Sterling Publishing Company, Inc.
387 Park Avenue South, New York, N.Y. 10016
© 2000 by Bob Bonnet and Dan Keen
Distributed in Canada by Sterling Publishing
℅ Canadian Manda Group, One Atlantic Avenue, Suite 105
Toronto, Ontario, Canada M6K 3E7
Distributed in Great Britain and Europe by Chris Lloyd
463 Ashley Road, Parkstone, Poole, Dorset, BH14 0AX, England
Distributed in Australia by Capricorn Link (Australia) Pty Ltd.
P.O. Box 6651, Baulkham Hills, Business Centre, NSW 2153, Australia
Manufactured in the United States of America

Sterling ISBN 0-8069-7771-X

CONTENTS

Introduction   5

Project

1 **Under Pressure** *How handling affects substances*   7
2 **Lemony Lineup** *Real lemon or fake food flavoring?*   8
3 **Nothing to Sniff At** *Smell and the secret of "wafting"*   10
4 **It's Litmus!** *Making pH (acid/base) testing strips*   11
5 **Acute Cuke** *The chemical change called pickling*   14
6 **Bad Cow?** *A non-taste test for sour milk*   15
7 **Less Is More** *For greater concentration, evaporate!*   16
8 **Cooking pHacts** *The effect of cooking on pH*   17
9 **Getting Ahead** *Reaction between a base and an acid*   18
10 **We Salute Solution** *Understanding basic chemical terms*   19
11 **Go, Old Mold!** *Food additives keep bread good longer*   20
12 **Captured Carbon** *The chemical reaction of burning*   22
13 **Tick Tock Tack** *Testing the oxidation time of metals*   24
14 **A Patch of White** *Green plants and photosynthesis*   25
15 **Pop Goes the Soda** *Reducing carbonation in soft drinks*   26
16 **How Electrifying!** *Examining the conduction of substances*   28
17 **We Deplore Pollution** *Water dilutes, but pollution remains*   30
18 **No Syrup** *The concept of viscosity*   32
19 **Egg Head** *Measuring endothermic reactions in eggs*   34
20 **One Candle Power** *Understanding exothermic reaction*   36
21 **Fade Not** *Natural dyes and sunlight*   38
22 **Sticky Goo!** *Emulsion, the "chem-magical" cleaner*   40
23 **Worth the Wait** *Unripe fruit to sugary treat*   42
24 **Sweeter Sweet** *Natural sugar or chemical substitute*   44
25 **Chemical Tears** *Overcoming an onion's natural gas*   46
26 **Saucy Cleaner** *A natural tarnish remover*   47
27 **The Yeast Beast** *Fermentation proves yeast is alive!*   48
28 **Better Bubbles** *Safe and natural monster-bubble solutions*   50
29 **Onion Switch** *Changing the taste of onions by cooking*   52
30 **Eaters' Digest** *Dissolving foods with acids*   53
31 **Left Behind** *It's in your water*   54

32 **Repeat, Threepeat** *Exact data allows repeatable results* 56
33 **Paint by Sugars** *Combining dyes* 58
34 **Colorful Disguise** *Smell and taste: team players* 60
35 **You've Changed!** *Identifying chemical and physical changes* 62
36 **Scent in a Cube** *Releasing fragrance with heat* 64
37 **Staying on Top** *Reduce a soap's density...and it floats!* 66
38 **Basic Building Blocks** *Getting to know the Periodic Table* 68
39 **Stressed Out** *The effects of weathering on elasticity* 70
40 **Heavy Gas, Man** *Releasing trapped gas to extinguish flame* 72
41 **Have a Taste, Bud** *Sugar sweetness a matter of chemistry* 74
42 **Settle Up** *Oil and water don't mix...usually* 76
43 **Building Blocks** *Growing natural crystal structures* 78
44 **Cool Clothes** *Testing for fabrics that "breathe"* 80
45 **Out of the Middle** *Separating liquids by density* 82
46 **Not Just Desserts** *Testing taste with combined flavors* 84
47 **Tricking the Brain** *When a food's color is changed* 86

Glossary 88

Index 93

INTRODUCTION

Welcome to the world of chemistry! This book explores projects in this fascinating field. Chemistry is the study of what substances are made of, how they can be changed and how they can be combined with other substances to make new substances. When substances are changed or combined, their old properties are changed and new ones are taken on. Plastic is an example of a new substance made from other substances.

Chemistry is a branch of physical science. It is one of the most interesting and motivating topics in science. It's important to understand chemistry because so many of its principles are found in other science disciplines, including astronomy, geology, mathematics, environmental science, botany, health and medicine, electronics, physics and even the arts. Some of its basic principles are safety, measurement, the scientific method of procedures and evaluation, cause and effect, written reporting of results and problem recognition.

Chemistry is at work all around us, and is a part of our daily lives. Medicines, garden fertilizers, food preservatives, synthetics, energy from batteries and the burning of coal to make electricity, glass made from limestone and sand, explosives, disinfectants for cleaning, and even the baking of yeast to cause bread to rise are all examples of chemistry at work. Read the label on packaged foods and cleaning supplies and you will often see listed the names of chemicals that are contained in it.

Energy can be given off from chemical changes: electricity, light and heat. When something burns, a chemical reaction is taking place, with light and heat given off. Chemical changes can occur when elements come in contact with each other, when they decompose or when temperature or pressure are changed.

Science Fair Projects

Because safety is and must always be the first consideration, we recommend that ALL activities be done under adult supervision. Even seemingly harmless objects can become a hazard under certain circumstances. If you can't do a project safely, then don't do it!

Respect for life should be fundamental. Your project cannot be inhumane to animals. Disruption of natural processes should not occur thoughtlessly and unnecessarily. Interference with ecological systems should always be avoided. Ethical rules must be followed also. It is unethical to hypothesize that one race or religion is better than another.

Science is the process of finding out. "The scientific method" is a procedure used by scientists and students in science fairs. It consists of several steps: identifying a problem or stating a purpose, forming a hypothesis, setting up an experiment to collect information, recording the results and coming to a conclusion as to whether or not the stated hypothesis is correct.

A science project starts by identifying a problem, asking a question or stating a purpose. The statement of the problem defines the boundaries of the investigation. For example, air pollution is a problem, but you must set the limits of your project. It is unlikely that you have access to an electron microscope, so an air pollution project could not check pollen in the air. This project might be limited to the accumulation of dust and other visible materials.

Once the problem is defined, a hypothesis (an educated guess about the results) must be formed. Hypothesize that there is more dust in a room that has thick carpeting than in a room that has hardwood or linoleum flooring.

Often, a hypothesis can be stated in more than one way. For example, in considering a project to gather data for using rocks to store and release heat during the night in a solar heated home, you might test to see if one large rock or many smaller rocks are better for giving off stored heat for a longer period of time. This could be stated in two ways: Hypothesize that one large rock will give off stored heat for a longer period of time than an equal mass of smaller rocks. Or, you could state the opposite: Hypothesize that smaller rocks will give off stored heat for a longer period of time compared to one large rock of equal mass. It does not matter which way the hypothesis is stated, nor does it matter which one is correct. The hypothesis doesn't have to be proven correct in order for the project to be a success; it is successful if facts are gathered and knowledge is gained.

Then you must set up an experiment to test your hypothesis. You will need to list materials, define the variables, constants and any assumptions, and document your procedure so that you or someone else will be able to repeat the experiment at another time. Finally, from the results collected, you must come to a conclusion as to whether or not the hypothesis is correct.

When choosing a science fair topic, pick something that is interesting to you, that you would like to work on. Then all of your research and study time will be spent on a subject you enjoy!

For presentation at a formal science fair, consider early on how you can demonstrate your project. Remember, you may not be able to control certain conditions in a gym or a hall. Decide how to display the project's steps and outcome, and keep a log or journal of how you got your results and came to your conclusion (photographs or even a video). Something hands-on or interactive often adds interest to a project display. As a fair-goer, what would *your* hands be itching to do? Now is the time to pass on some of that enjoyment.

Bob Bonnet & Dan Keen

Project 1
Under Pressure
How handling affects substances

Purpose Studying the effects of squeezing on liquid, a solid, some gel and a colloidal substance.

Overview Pressure sometimes causes a change in matter. Great underground pressure is what creates diamonds. But even squeezing by hand can cause change in certain substances. Cornstarch, made from corn and used in cooking as a thickening agent (as in gravy), is what is called a colloidal substance. It is made up of small particles that don't dissolve but stay suspended in a fluid. Mixed with water, when cornstarch is at rest, it forms a substance that somewhat resembles a liquid, but the substance changes its property to be more like a solid when pressure is applied.

You need
- cornstarch
- teaspoon
- water
- gelatin dessert
- piece of ice

Hypothesis Of four sample materials, only the colloidal substance will undergo physical change (other than breaking up) when hand pressure is applied.

Procedure Take some gelatin dessert from the refrigerator, place it into the palm of your hand and use the forefinger and thumb of your other hand to apply pressure. The CONSTANT is the application of this pinching pressure. The VARIABLES are the materials being tested. Now, apply pressure to an ice chip or cube, and to some water.

Next, shake about a teaspoon of cornstarch into your palm. Add a few drops of water to the cornstarch, and stir it around to mix it in. Slowly add a few more drops, a little at a time. When the mixture is slightly watery, it's ready. Now, squeeze the colloidal substance between your forefinger and thumb and the pressure causes it to become putty-like. Stop, and it becomes more liquid, with a little water seeping into your palm. Do it again. Doesn't it have a strange feel? What a great natural toy!

Results & Conclusion Write down the results of your experiment. Come to a conclusion as to whether or not your hypothesis was correct.

Something more Does a flour-and-water mixture become a colloidal substance?

Project 2
Lemony Lineup
Real lemon or fake food flavoring?

Purpose Can the natural flavor of a fresh-squeezed lemon in water be recognized in a lineup when compared to a drink made from frozen or lemon drink "concentrate" or an artificially flavored lemonade?

Overview Through chemical research, substances have been created that smell or taste like other natural substances—and even more so! Often, it's these substances, rather than the actual items, that are used in manufactured and food products to make the products more appealing to the consumer.

You need
   a can of frozen lemonade
   concentrate, or container
   of lemonade made from
   concentrate
- artificial-flavoring lemonade
   drink (no lemon ingredient)
- a lemon
- water
- 3 drinking glasses

If you have ever been in the kind of store that sells leather goods such as pocket books, attaché cases, travel luggage, or saddles, you may have noticed a strong scent of leather. It could be the real smell of the leather or it could be a case of chemical trickery, where the products, real leather or not, have been chemically treated to make them smell more "leathery." Maybe the leather scent was even just sprayed into the air! Is that great smell of apples and cinnamon in your local bakery real? Is baking actually done on the premises?

People tend to associate the smell of lemon with cleanliness and freshness. That's why, on supermarket shelves, you will find dish detergents, laundry detergents and liquid bathroom cleaners that have a lemon scent. Although the products smell like lemon, they very likely don't really have lemon juice in them at all.

In the same way, manufacturers will sometimes place flavoring additives in their products, to make them taste even more like the fruit they are supposed to contain, "even fruitier" than the fruit would be by itself. Are you surprised to think that a drink that has been artificially flavored may taste more "real" than a drink made from the real fruit? Read the ingredients listed on your favorite drinks. Does the grape drink really have grape juice listed as an ingredient? Is it mostly water (the higher-quantity substances are listed first) or other less flavorful juices? Has grape or other flavoring been added? Look at the ingredients listed on powdered drink mixes, too.

Hypothesis A drink made with a lemon concentrate and/or artificially flavored lemonade mix will taste more "lemony" than one made with the juice of fresh-squeezed lemon.

Procedure For the project, prepare three "lemonades." First, using a can of frozen lemonade concentrate, add water and mix according to the instructions...or simply pour some from a container of "made from concentrate" lemon drink.

Next, pour some artificially flavored lemon drink from a container, or mix up a serving from a packet of artificial lemonade mix that needs water added to it. Read the labels on the containers, cans or packets, to be sure you are using the right thing. Here, look for the phrase "artificial flavoring." Pour some into a drinking glass.

Carefully cut a lemon in half, squeeze some of the juice into a drinking glass and add a little water to it. (You might want to add a tiny bit of sugar, too.) Stir.

Do a taste test. If the real lemon drink tastes weak, too watery, squeeze out more lemon juice. You want to taste the lemon. The CONSTANT is your body's taste system. The VARIABLE is the source of the lemon flavor.

Which drink tastes more lemony to you: the juice from a fresh lemon, lemonade made from concentrate, or artificially flavored lemonade?

Results & Conclusion Write down the results of your experiment. Come to a conclusion as to whether or not your hypothesis was correct.

Something more
1. Have your friends and family members taste each of the three drinks, without them knowing the source of each juice. Do they come to the same conclusion that you did?
2. Would the results be any different if other juices were compared? Try orange or lime.

Project 3

Nothing to Sniff At

Smell and the secret of "wafting"

Purpose How to smell a strong substance safely.

Overview Smells come from in-air particles in the form of gases and vapors. The chemical solution and nerve cells that line our noses interact with the vapors, and the brain interprets the smell.

> **You need**
> • an adult
> • onion
> • knife
> • small closeable plastic bag

Although some scents, like flowers, cinnamon, and coffee, are nice, others are unpleasant and can even be hazardous. Breathing gas, for example, given off by powdered chlorine granules used in swimming pools when even a little water is spilled on them, can make you deathly ill. *Never* inhale, or take a deep breath, of any substance that you are not perfectly sure is completely safe!

A safety practice in chemistry of just "sampling" a scent, which should be used throughout your life, is called wafting. It's a way to get just a "whiff" of the odor a substance gives off. A very small amount is mixed, with a wave of your hand, into a puff of air—then you quickly "sniff."

Hypothesis You can "sample" an odor in a way that avoids physical discomfort.

Procedure This science project demonstrates the seriousness, and danger, of breathing in substances. The CONSTANT is the human olfactory system—the nose. The VARIABLE is the method used to introduce the onion odor to your nose.

First, have an adult chop up a strong fresh onion and close it in a plastic bag. Open the bag near your face. Quickly wave your hand over the opening, fanning some of the onion vapors past your nose. Sniff, and close the bag. Did you smell the onion? Now open the bag and take in a good deep breath. You'll probably cough and your eyes will tear up. Which do you think is the safer way to smell the vapor?

Results & Conclusion Write down the results of your experiment. Come to a conclusion as to whether or not your hypothesis was correct.

Something more Try wafting other unpleasant-smelling, *safe* (food) substances.

Project 4

It's Litmus!

Making pH (acid/base) testing strips

Purpose Learning the best way to make home-made litmus testing papers for experimenting.

Overview One characteristic of chemical substances is the amount of acid or base they contain. Foods that contain weak acids, for example, lemon or lime juice and pickles, taste sour. On the pH scale, the opposite of acid is base, also called alkali. Bases have a slippery feel and taste bitter. Examples of base substances are milk of magnesia, baking soda, soap, ammonia, and many cleaners. Both strong acids and bases may be very hazardous; they can burn and hurt you. Powerful cleaning products, especially those that unclog household drains, contain very strong bases that can be hazardous if they get on your skin or are breathed in.

> **You need**
> • an adult
> • wax paper
> • a red cabbage
> • large pot, to heat cabbage
> • water
> • use of stove
> • plain white paper towel
> • lemon juice
> • baking soda

In the way a ruler is used to measure how long something is and a thermometer is used to show how hot something is, chemists use the pH scale as a measurement of the amount of acid or base a substance contains. The technical term pH comes from "the **p**otential of power + **H**ydrogen." Chemists have a meter that can measure pH electronically, but that is not how pH was measured long ago, and we can still do it this original, easier way.

The pH scale goes from 0 to 14, 0 being the strongest acid, 7 being neutral (in the middle) and 14 the strongest base, or alkali. Pure water has a pH of 7. If you have a swimming pool, you may have used pH testing, where a sample of water is collected and a few drops of a special chemical are added and mixed together. The resulting color of the water is matched against a color comparison chart to find the exact pH.

Note: The information in this project serves as a background for the following few projects, which also work with pH, acids and bases.

One way to measure pH is by using litmus paper. Litmus paper comes in different colors to measure different ranges of pH. Red litmus paper turns blue in a base solution. Blue litmus paper turns red in an acid solution. A color chart is used to compare the color litmus paper turns to a pH number.

Hypothesis Hypothesize that homemade litmus paper can be made from the juice of a red cabbage, and for best results the juice should be concentrated.

Procedure Litmus paper is inexpensive and can be purchased at a science shop or through a science catalog, but you can also make your own. Have an adult help you boil a red cabbage (the kind of cabbage that is purple in color). It should be cut into quarters, placed in a pot with a cupful of water, and boiled. After about fifteen to twenty minutes, turn off the stove.

Cut some plain white paper toweling into small strips. When the pot's contents have cooled, transfer the cabbage water to a glass and dip several strips into it. Place them on wax paper to dry.

Now we want to make a second batch of strips by dipping them into cabbage water that is more concentrated to see if the stronger liquid will make the litmus strips react and change color more clearly. The paper toweling and the evaluation materials (the lemon juice and baking soda) are the CONSTANTS. The VARIABLE is the concentration of the cabbage water.

For the second batch of strips, let the cabbage water sit in the glass for several days in a warm, sunny spot in your home until a lot of the water has evaporated. This will mean the cabbage water that remains is more concentrated. Dip strips of paper towel into this concentrated solution and lay them on wax paper to dry.

Use your homemade litmus paper to test lemon juice (an acid) and baking soda mixed in water (a base). What color does your homemade litmus paper turn when

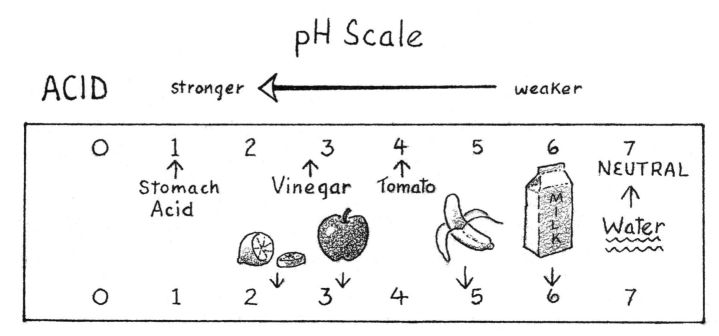

a few drops of lemon juice are placed on it? What color does the litmus paper turn when a few drops of baking soda mixed in water are placed on it? Do strips from the second batch of litmus paper change color more clearly than those from the first, and so make a better indicator?

Results & Conclusion Write down the results of your experiment. Come to a conclusion as to whether or not your hypothesis was correct.

Something more

1. In addition to making litmus paper, simply pour ¼ cup of the cabbage water into three glasses. Add a little baking soda to one glass and some lemon juice to another. Watch the color changes. Compare the two colors to the original color.

2. Make your own color comparison chart for use with your homemade litmus paper. See the pH scale chart shown at the bottom of these pages. The pH numbers are given for different items such as vinegar, bananas, and milk of magnesia.

weaker ————————⟶ stronger   BASE

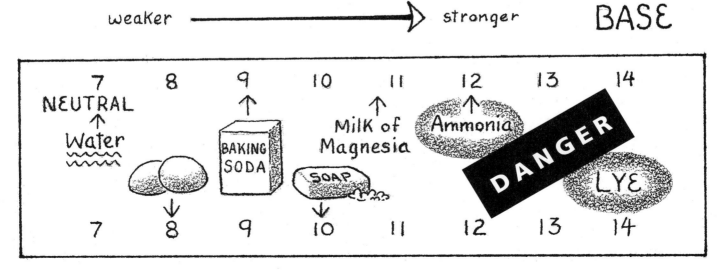

| 7 | 8 | 9 | 10 | 11 | 12 | 13 | 14 |

NEUTRAL
Water

BAKING SODA

Milk of Magnesia

SOAP

Ammonia

DANGER

LYE

| 7 | 8 | 9 | 10 | 11 | 12 | 13 | 14 |

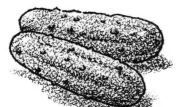

Project 5

Acute Cuke

The chemical change called pickling

Purpose Some like sweet pickles, some like sour ones, some prefer regular cucumbers. What's the difference in their pH readings?

Overview Pickling is a chemical process used to preserve food. Fruits, vegetables and even meats can be pickled. The food to be preserved is soaked in vinegar and brine (brine is very salty water). Sometimes sugar and spices are added to change the flavor.

You need
- dill pickle
- fresh cucumber
- litmus paper
- color comparison chart for litmus paper
- 2 spoons

The most common food that is processed that way is the cucumber, which is then called a "pickle." Dill pickles are the most common type of sour-tasting pickles. Small pickled cucumbers, called gherkins, are known for their sweet taste.

Does a food that tastes sour have a low pH, meaning it is an acid? (Refer to the detailed explanations of pH and litmus paper in the glossary and in Project #4.)

Hypothesis Hypothesize that a sour-tasting pickle will have a low pH.

Procedure Squeeze some cucumber juice onto a spoon and some pickle juice onto another spoon. Use a strip of litmus paper to test the pH of the cucumber juice, then the juice of the dill pickle. Which is more acidic? Which tastes more sour? The CONSTANTS are your taste buds and the litmus paper pH indicators. The VARIABLE is the state of the cucumber—fresh or dilled.

Results & Conclusion Write down the results of your experiment. Come to a conclusion as to whether or not your hypothesis was correct.

Something more Do sweeter pickles, such as gherkins, have low pH? Test several kinds of pickle after hypothesizing which will have lower pH. Then eat them.

Project 6

Bad Cow?

A non-taste test for sour milk

Purpose Milk may smell okay, but is it? We need a way to see if milk is bad without tasting it.

Overview Milk is kept in the refrigerator so it will keep fresh longer. When it sours, an acid is formed. Since no one likes to get a mouthful of sour milk, can we find out if milk is still good by testing instead of tasting it? (Smelling the milk sometimes works—but not always.) Since an acid forms in sour milk, how about checking its pH?

You need
- milk
- 2 glasses
- litmus paper (blue-dyed best for acid testing)
- color comparison chart
- several days' time

Hypothesis Hypothesize that you can tell if milk is sour by using pH testing.

Procedure Pour some fresh milk into a glass. Use litmus paper to check its pH and write it down. Now let the milk sit at room temperature for a few days. Once a day, use litmus paper to check the pH of the left-out milk. The CONSTANT is the litmus paper used as a pH indicator. The VARIABLE is the milk.

After a number of days, pour some fresh milk into another glass and test them both. Compare the pH of the fresh glass of milk to the original pH test on the first glass. Is it the same…or nearly? (The refrigerated milk may also not be as fresh as it was some days ago.) Observe the condition of the milk that had been left out and compare it to the newly poured milk. Does it look different? Smell different? If you are not sure you see a difference, leave the "old" milk out another day or two. Does milk that has spoiled measure as more acid?

Results & Conclusion Write down the results of your experiment. Come to a conclusion as to whether or not your hypothesis was correct.

Something more Do foods like hot pepper sauce and horseradish taste "hot" because they have a low pH?

Project 7
Less Is More

For greater concentration, evaporate!

Purpose To find out if an acidic liquid increases in acidity from concentration due to evaporation.

Overview When water in a solution evaporates, what is left in the liquid becomes more concentrated. A pool of salt water becomes saltier; the amount of salt stays the same but is less diluted.

During a hot dry spell, the sodium, calcium and pollutants in the waters of ponds, lakes and tide pools can become more concentrated, where no new water is added. This may put a strain on the plant and animal life that live there.

As evaporation takes place and the water remaining becomes more concentrated, is there a change in pH?

You need
- litmus paper
- color comparison chart
- drinking glass
- lemon juice
- water
- spoon
- a sunny window
- several days' time

Hypothesis Hypothesize that pH change is measurable as liquid evaporates.

Procedure Pour several spoonfuls of lemon juice into a drinking glass. Fill the rest of the glass with water. Stir. Using litmus paper and a color comparison chart, determine the pH of the solution. Is this solution an acid or a base?

Place the glass in a sunny window until only about a third of the solution is left. Check the pH again. Has it changed? Has the solution become stronger, that is, more acidic (a lower pH number)? The CONSTANT is the room environment and the litmus paper test strips. The VARIABLE is the liquid as it becomes more concentrated.

Results & Conclusion Write down the results of your experiment. Come to a conclusion as to whether or not your hypothesis was correct.

Something more
1. Would the lemon juice itself, composed mostly of water, evaporate and become more concentrated? Could this be measured by a change in pH?
2. Compare the pH difference of fresh-squeezed lemon juice and bottled concentrate.

16

Project 8

Cooking pHacts

The effect of cooking on pH

Purpose To find out if the process of cooking changes a food's pH.

Overview Foods can change quite a bit when they are cooked. Some taste differently than when they are raw. (A friend who likes to eat bell peppers that are cooked, such as "stuffed pepper" for dinner, can't stand to eat them raw, in a salad.)

Sometimes cooking removes vitamins from a food. This is especially true of water-soluble vitamins (vitamin C, for example). Does cooking also change the pH of foods?

Hypothesis Hypothesize that the pH of onion juice is changed by cooking.

You need
- an adult
- onion
- litmus paper
- color comparison chart
- a bowl
- garlic press
- cooking pot
- use of stove

Procedure Peel an onion. Using a garlic press, squeeze some pieces of onion and catch the juice in a bowl. Determine the pH of the onion juice with litmus paper and a color comparison chart.

Pour the juice into a small cooking pot and slowly bring it to a boil. Be careful working around a hot stove. Be sure to have an adult present for safety. As soon as the juice boils, turn the stove burner off and let the pot and juice cool. When cool, measure the pH again. Has it changed? The litmus paper used as a pH indicator is CONSTANT. The onion is the VARIABLE, cooked or raw.

Results & Conclusion Write down the results of your experiment. Come to a conclusion as to whether or not your hypothesis was correct.

Something more Try checking the pH of other liquids and then bringing them to a boil to see if cooking affects pH. Use a solution of baking soda and water (which is a base) and then test lemon juice (which is an acid).

Project 9
Getting Ahead

Reaction between a base and an acid

Purpose Can lemon juice replace vinegar in the traditional "volcano eruption" project?

Overview When baking soda and vinegar come together, a chemical reaction takes place. (Baking soda is a "base" and vinegar is an "acid.") Carbon dioxide gas, known as CO_2, is quickly released. Bubbles foam up and spill out of the container in a violent eruption that's impressive but an all-too-common project. But, is there something special about vinegar that causes this reaction, or is it simply the fact that vinegar is an acid?

> **You need**
> • baking soda
> • lemon juice
> • vinegar
> • 2 same-size drinking glasses
> • teaspoon
> • a sink

Hypothesis Because vinegar and lemon juice are both acids, their reactions to baking soda will be similar.

Procedure Pour some vinegar into one glass and the same amount of lemon juice into the other. Holding the glass with vinegar over a sink, add a teaspoonful of baking soda. A chemical reaction takes place, releasing CO_2—like opening a soda can that has been shaken. Notice the size of the bubble "head."

Then, hold the glass with the lemon juice—an acid, too—over the sink. Add the teaspoonful of baking soda. The baking soda is CONSTANT. The VARIABLE is the type of acids used, vinegar and lemon juice. Does the lemon juice solution bubble?

Results & Conclusion Write down the results of your experiment. Come to a conclusion as to whether or not your hypothesis was correct.

Something more
1. Try other substances with acid pH: orange, grapefruit, other citrus juices. Check their pHs first. Is the reaction bigger with lower pH juices (more/less acidic)?
2. Does temperature affect the reaction of acid and baking soda? Put some pH acid in the refrigerator and an equal amount in a warm, sunny window. Once temperatures have adjusted, add an equal amount of baking soda and observe the reactions.

Project 10

We Salute Solution

Understanding basic chemical terms

Purpose "Solutes" and "solvents" can chemically combine, other substances don't. True?

Overview A "mixture" is two or more substances mixed together which do not chemically combine but remain the same as before. In a solution, a substance (called a solute) dissolves, becoming evenly distributed throughout another substance (called a solvent).

You need
- salt
- pepper
- water
- 2 drinking glasses
- teaspoon

Hypothesis Hypothesize that pepper, which is not a solute, does not chemically combine with water. Salt, however, will combine with water.

Procedure Add a teaspoon of salt to a drinking glass filled with water. Stir. The salt dissolves into the water and can no longer be seen nor easily removed. The water and salt have chemically combined to form a "solution."

Add a teaspoon of pepper to another glass filled with water. Stir. Has the pepper dissolved in the water, or is it floating on top or rising slowly within it? Has the pepper stayed essentially the way it was before it was added to the water? Pepper and water make a "mixture." The water and the amount of material added to the water are CONSTANT. The type of material added to the water is varied (salt, then pepper).

Results & Conclusion Write down the results of your experiment. Come to a conclusion as to whether or not your hypothesis was correct.

Something more
1. Can you add salt to a glass of water until so much is added that no more will dissolve into the water, and the salt instead settles to the bottom of the glass?
2. You can separate pepper from water by skimming it off the surface. Is it possible to recover salt from water? What if the water were evaporated?
3. Adding powdered chocolate to warm milk to make hot cocoa is a solution. Does adding sugar to iced tea make a solution or a mixture?

Project 11

Go, Old Mold!

Food additives keep bread good longer

Purpose Determine which brands and types of bread you buy have chemical mold inhibitors added to them.

Overview A science experiment traditionally done in elementary school grades involves growing mold on a slice of moist bread. Molds are microscopic plants. Molds grow from tiny particles called spores, which travel through the air. A moist slice of bread is an excellent "home" for mold to grow.

However, in recent years teachers are finding that growing mold on bread isn't always easy! The reason is that many breads today have some kind of special chemical added to them to stop mold. It is called a mold inhibitor.

Food additives are substances added to foods during processing to either help preserve them, improve color or flavor, or make their texture more appealing. Chemists have also devised food additives that inhibit (slow down) the growth of molds, and some of those additives are commonly placed in packaged bread. These food additives have passed many tests and have been approved by the United States Food and Drug Administration as being safe to eat before manufacturers were permitted to add them to their food products.

By adding such mold-inhibitor chemicals to breads, today's baked loaves will not go moldy and will remain edible for a longer period of time.

Does fresh-baked bread from a local bakery provide a better medium (place)

> **You need**
> - packaged white bread
> - fresh white bread (home-baked or local bakery)
> - rye bread
> - wheat bread
> - water
> - four plates
> - teaspoon
> - pencil
> - paper

for growing mold than mass-processed, packaged bread from a supermarket, which may contain food additives as preservatives?

Hypothesis   Hypothesize that some breads are made with mold inhibitors added, so mold will not grow on them as quickly as on other breads.

Procedure   Select four slices of bread and place each on a plate. Each slice should be a different kind of bread. One slice should be from a fresh-baked loaf from a local bakery. One should be a packaged white bread, another a slice of rye bread and another a slice of wheat bread. You may also wish to test oat-nut bread, a multigrain bread, or any other interesting bread you find at the store or is home-baked.

Set the plates in an out-of-the-way place. Every day, sprinkle three drops of water on each slice of bread to keep them moist. Write down your observations about each slice of bread every day. How long is it before you see mold forming? Which bread is the first to begin growing mold? Which is the last?

For your report, ask your local bakery if it uses any preservative or mold-inhibitor food additives in the bread you used in your project. Compare the lists of ingredients of each loaf of packaged bread you tested.

Results & Conclusion   Write down the results of your experiment. Come to a conclusion as to whether or not your hypothesis was correct.

Something more
1. Hypothesize that keeping bread cooler will also help preserve it. Repeat the above experiment, but place an additional slice of each bread in the refrigerator. Check all the breads once a day and write down your observations.
2. One possible variable in the "something more" experiment above that wasn't controlled was light. The slice of bread *in the refrigerator* did not have light. Was it the temperature or the absence of light that affected the mold test results?
3. If spores get onto the bread from the air, would placing a slice of bread that gets moldy quickly inside a piece of clear plastic wrap keep it from getting moldy?

Project 12

Captured Carbon

The chemical reaction of burning

Purpose Is it possible to detect and display the carbon given off from a burning candle?

Overview Oxidation is a process that occurs when oxygen combines chemically with other substances and changes them. Oxidation can happen quickly: wax oxidizes rapidly on a burning candle. Oxidation can happen slowly: an iron object oxidizes as it turns to rust.

When oxidation occurs fast, heat is given off quickly and sometimes light is given off, too. When a wooden log burns in a fireplace, the log is oxidizing rapidly, giving off heat and light.

Carbon is also a result of burning. Carbon is one of the basic elements of matter. It combines with many other substances to take on different forms. Diamonds are carbon. Gasoline and even beets contain carbon. Carbon can combine with oxygen to form carbon dioxide, which is a gas that plants absorb to make food for the plant.

> You need
> • an adult
> • candle
> • candle holder
> • matches
> • dinner plate
> • piece of paper toweling

Hypothesis Hypothesize that light and heat are not the only things given off by a burning candle; that carbon is given off, too, as a result of the rapid oxidation taking place.

Procedure We can prove the hypothesis by capturing some of the carbon being produced as a candle burns.

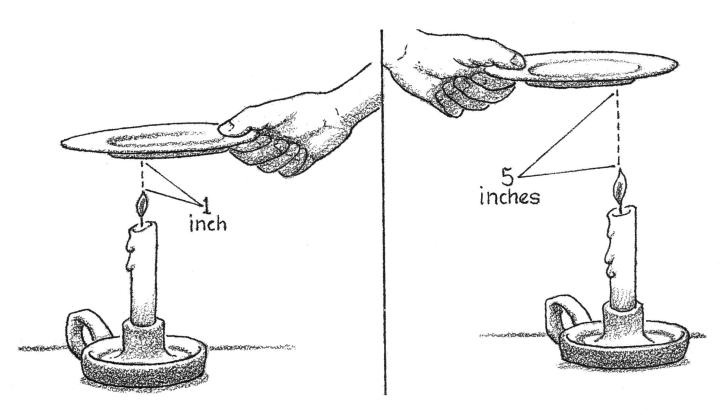

Place a candle securely in a candle holder on a high table. Have an adult light a candle and stand by to help. Then, grasp a china dinner plate or bowl by its edge. Be sure that the dish is made of china, ceramic or a similar material that does not burn (do not use a paper or plastic plate). Use caution around the lit candle.

Looking at the candle flame, hold the dish so the center of it is just about an inch (2.5 cm) above the flame tip. Hold it there for only several seconds. Do not hold the plate over the flame too long or it might become too hot to hold.

Observe the bottom of the dish. Is it turning black as carbon is collected? Hold the dish away from the candle until it cools and can be touched. Rub your finger across the black carbon that has been captured on the plate. Notice how it easily wipes off the plate and onto your finger. Use a paper towel to clean your hand, and be sure to wash the plate.

Hold the plate over the candle again, this time keeping it about five inches (12 cm) from the tip of the flame. Does carbon build up as quickly? Carbon builds up, laying on itself. Can you collect more carbon by holding the plate close to the tip of the flame, or farther away? The CONSTANT is the burning candle. The VARIABLE is the distance of the dish from the flame.

Extinguish the candle flame when you are done.

Results & Conclusion   Write down the results of your experiment. Come to a conclusion as to whether or not your hypothesis was correct.

Something more   Could you use the collected carbon for face painting at a party or for doing artwork?

Project 13

Tick Tock Tack

Testing the oxidation time of metals

Purpose   What materials become oxidized.

Overview   Oxidation is a process that occurs when oxygen combines with various substances. As explained in the last project, oxidation can occur rapidly, like when a candle burns; or take a long time, like when iron rusts.

If you wished to tack up posters or hang holiday decorations outdoors, you'd want to be sure the thumbtacks or push pins would hold up well in the weather.

Hypothesis   Hypothesize which items in water will rust.

Procedure   Find several kinds of thumbtacks. Some may be coated, some may be brass. Place the tacks along with a push pin in a clear jar filled with water. A mayonnaise, peanut butter or pickle jar will work well. The jar may be plastic or glass.

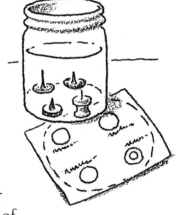

Draw a diagram on a piece of paper showing the location of each thumbtack and the name of its brand. Set the jar in an out-of-the-way place. Once a day, look at the objects in the jar and write down your observations. The water and the period of time under test is the CONSTANT. The VARIABLE is the different materials being tested.

After one week, examine your notes on the observations you made. Which one started to rust first? Are there any that did not rust? Why do you think some did not rust as much as others?

Results & Conclusion   Write down the results of your experiment. Come to a conclusion as to whether or not your hypothesis was correct.

Something more   Try using other types of metal objects, such as staples and brass fasteners. Make daily observations and note any changes.

Project 14

A Patch of White

Green plants and photosynthesis

Purpose Will chlorophyll return to grass that has been deprived of light? Let's figure it out.

Overview Chlorophyll is a chemical in plants that makes them green. With the help of light energy, a plant's chlorophyll turns carbon dioxide and water into sugars it uses for food (the process of photosynthesis) and causes oxygen to be released. If a plant doesn't get the light it needs, photosynthesis can't take place and the plant loses its green coloring. If such a patch of grass is later opened to sunlight again, will the blades of white grass recover…turn green again?

You need
- a patch a green grass
- 3 foot square piece of plywood
- several weeks' time
- pencil
- paper

Hypothesis Decide whether you think white blades of grass do recover and turn green again, or if they wither and die and new green grass grows from the roots.

Procedure To test your hypothesis, lay a piece of plywood over a section of green grass in a sunny area. Every day, lift up the plywood for a moment and observe the color of the grass underneath. Write down your observations. Is the green color becoming paler? Compare it to the color of the surrounding grass. The patch of grass remains CONSTANT. The VARIABLE is the light reaching the grass.

When the patch of grass has become white-looking, remove the plywood and leave it off. Every day, look at the grass patch and write down your observations. Does photosynthesis begin again in the blades of grass once the light has returned?

Results & Conclusion Write down the results of your experiment. Come to a conclusion as to whether or not your hypothesis was correct.

Something more If blades of grass do not recover once they turn white, would they start photosynthesis again if the length of time sunlight was kept from them was reduced? How can you test and show this?

Project 15

Pop Goes the Soda

Reducing carbonation in soft drinks

Purpose How can we minimize the amount of carbon dioxide ingested from drinking a carbonated soda.

Overview In 1772 in England, Joseph Priestly was trying to discover how to imitate the natural bubbling waters of some mineral springs. That was the beginning of what is done today in many popular drinks. The ingredient that gives soda, sparkling water and other such drinks their bubbly taste is carbon dioxide (chemical symbol CO_2). It makes a soda tickle your mouth and nose when you drink it.

When you breathe out, carbon dioxide is exhaled. Carbon dioxide gas is also formed by burning things that have the element carbon in them, which includes wood, coal and oil (In Project 12, carbon was collected from the gas of a burning candle.) Trees and plants take in carbon dioxide and release oxygen. This cycle is nature's way of providing clean air for people and animals to breathe, as well as carbon dioxide for trees and plants.

Carbon dioxide can be put under pressure and added to drinks to give them a pleasant biting taste and bubbly appearance. When carbon dioxide is added to

> **You need**
> - 2 20-ounce plastic bottles of soda
> - 2 gallon-size sealable clear plastic food bags
> - a sunny window
> - use of freezer
> - clock or watch

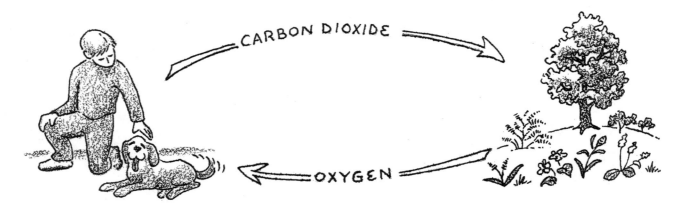

water it is called soda water. Soft drinks (often called soda pop, or simply soda or pop) have become a big part of our society. They are called soft drinks to distinguish them from beverages containing alcohol (hard drinks). Can you imagine having a barbecue without soda to drink?

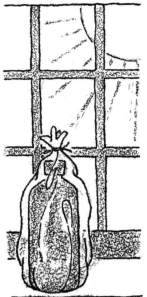

Although the carbon dioxide in our drinks is not harmful, the bubbles may cause gas in your stomach, which could cause some discomfort. If you wanted to minimize the amount of carbon dioxide that you ingest, would it be better to drink your soda cold or warm it up, open the cap, then cool it before drinking?

An interesting historical note: Soft drinks are also called "pop" because the bottle caps used prior to the 1890s made a popping noise when removed from the bottle.

Hypothesis   Hypothesize which of two bottles of soda will give off more carbon dioxide when opened, as detected by the sound of escaping gas when their caps are finally unsealed.

Procedure   Place a 20-ounce bottle of soda in a clear plastic food bag, one that can be sealed. Similarly, place another 20-ounce bottle of the same kind of soda in a plastic bag. Set one soda in the freezer section of a refrigerator. Set the other soda in a sunny window. Wait one hour (*no longer!*—we do *not* want the soda in the freezer to freeze).

Place the two sodas on a table, keeping them in the sealed bags. Unscrew the cap off of each by grasping the cap through the sealed bag. The CONSTANTS are the type and amount of soda. The temperature is the VARIABLE.

Which soda made the loudest "hissing" sound as gas escaped when the cap was opened? Which one spilled out the most gas and soda? The soda which made the loudest hiss and pushed out the most liquid now has less carbonated gas in it. If you drank that one, there would be less gas in your stomach. If it was the warm soda, you could now pour it in a glass, add ice to make it more desirable to drink, and it would put less gas in your stomach.

Results & Conclusion   Write down the results of your experiment. Come to a conclusion as to whether or not your hypothesis was correct.

Something more
1. Would the color of soda affect results? Repeat the experiment using a clear-colored soda (or use a dark-colored soda if you did the experiment first with a clear-colored soda).
2. Does shaking a bottle before opening it cause it to release more gas when the cap is unsealed? (Do this outside or in a container, so as not to splatter soda on your clothing or other objects around you.)

Project 16
How Electrifying!
Examining the conduction of substances

Purpose Learning what common materials are good conductors of electricity.

Overview Substances are described by color, texture, smell, feel and hardness. Another characteristic might be an ability to conduct electricity.

Gather some common items (see "needs" list): metal coins made of basic elements like copper, gold and silver jewelry, a plastic comb (or other item made from a chemical process using oil).

A battery is used to store electricity (a chemical reaction takes place within the battery). Electricity flows from the negative terminal on one battery to the positive one of another following a path, such as a piece of wire. The material used for the path is called a conductor. An electrical conductor is any material that allows an electric current to flow through it easily. Metal is a good conductor. Copper is used as a conductor in some phone wires, computers and other electronic appliances.

When a conductor provides a path between the negative terminal on a battery and the positive terminal, electricity flows through the conductor. Think of the flow of electricity as if it were flowing water. A metal wire carries the electric flow, just as pipes carry water flow. If we put something in the path of the electric current, the current will try to flow through the object. If that substance is a conductor, the current will flow through. If it is not a good conductor, little or no current will flow through. By placing a light bulb in the path, we can see when current is flowing in the wire, since the current will light the bulb as it flows through it.

Hypothesis Hypothesize which gathered materials are good electrical conductors.

You need
- brass fastener
- coins (penny, nickel, dime, quarter)
- plant stem
- twig from a tree
- teabag
- water
- gold ring or necklace
- piece of silver jewelry
- nail
- plastic comb
- insulated jumper leads with alligator clips at each end
- dual "D"-cell battery holder
- 2 batteries (1.5 volt "D" size)
- flashlight bulb
- bulb socket

Procedure   The battery and light bulb conductivity tester we will construct is the CONSTANT. The VARIABLES are the types of material being tested.

At your local electronic parts store, you should have been able to find two "D"-cell flashlight batteries, a dual "D"-cell battery holder, a flashlight bulb, a socket for the bulb and a set of insulated jumper leads with alligator clips on each end. The alligator-clip leads make it quick and easy to connect all the components together, and to clip onto the different materials we want to test as conductors. Using those alligator clip leads, connect the components together as shown below. Be sure to place the batteries in the holder correctly, each one facing a different direction. The two batteries used together make 3 volts (each is 1.5 volts and 1.5 + 1.5 = 3).

The battery holder must be one with a wire running from positive terminal (raised "+" end) on one battery to the negative terminal (flat "−" end) on the other to form an electrical path. This connection is made at the opposite end of the battery holder from where the alligator clips are attached. If the holder you have doesn't have this connection, a 3-inch-long strip of aluminum foil ½ inch wide can be placed inside the battery holder, touching the positive end of one battery terminal to the negative end of the other.

The path is completed by clipping a coin between the two alligator clips. Does the bulb light up? Now unclip the coin and, in turn, clip on the other things you've collected (coins, a twig, nail, plastic comb). Make two piles, one of electrical conductors and one of nonconductors.

Note: In a science fair, avoid possible theft from an unattended display by leaving expensive jewelry or coins at home.

Results & Conclusion   Write down the results of your experiment. Come to a conclusion as to whether or not your hypothesis was correct.

Something more

It's interesting to note that many household items that do not conduct electricity (called insulators) can build up static electricity—a balloon, wool sweater, comb made from plastic, and glass stirring-rod, for example. Static electricity is a buildup of electrons. Try to build up a static charge on these items. Hold a balloon against the screen of a television set. Take a wool sweater out of a clothes dryer. Run a plastic comb through your hair when it's very dry. Check the items on the conductor tester you constructed in the above experiment and prove that these items do not conduct electric current, even though they can hold a static electrical charge.

Project 17

We Deplore Pollution

Water dilutes, but pollution remains

Purpose A trace (an extremely small amount) of a solute in a solvent may not be detectable by taste.

Overview Just a few drops of an unwanted substance can ruin another substance. A little pollution in pure water can make it undrinkable. Just imagine how few molecules of a substance are necessary for air to carry and spread them. When cookies or a cake is baking in the oven, you can smell it all through the house. Yet, such a small amount of cake is lost to the air that it isn't measurable by us.

For a while, some people thought that unclean water could be cleaned by diluting it (making it weaker). The popular saying was, "The solution to pollution is dilution." Environmentalists now know that just isn't true. That is why everyone must be responsible, so as not to pollute our environment. It may be difficult or even impossible to make water clean and drinkable once certain substances have been mixed into it.

Even if something is diluted, it can still remain contaminated. Even if we cannot taste or see something in the water, that doesn't mean that it is not there. Prove this by using sugar and water.

Hypothesis Hypothesize you can't detect a trace amount of sugar when it is heavily diluted in water. Being aware of this shows how important it is for us to be environmentally wise and keep water from becoming polluted.

Procedure   Fill a clean, empty one-gallon jug with tap water. The jug may originally have held milk or mineral water. Then fill a drinking glass with the same water.

Add a very, very small amount of sugar to the water in the jug, only about $1/8$ of a teaspoon. Put the cap on the jug and shake it. Wipe the mouth of the jug with a towel to be sure there are no granules of sugar on it. Pour a little into a glass and take a sip. Do you taste any sweetness from the sugar you put in? Take a drink of the glass of plain water and compare the taste. The water is CONSTANT. The VARIABLE is the water which contains a trace amount of sugar.

Even though you may not taste any sweetness, the sugar is still present in the water. The sugar is very diluted (weak), but it is there, making the water not completely pure. You know the sugar is in there, because you put it in.

This shows that even though we may not be able to detect the presence of a substance because it is not there in sufficiently large amount, some of the substance could still be present.

Water may meet all of the government regulations for drinkable water, but that water may still have some contaminants in it that may not be healthy for us to drink.

Results & Conclusion   Write down the results of your experiment. Come to a conclusion as to whether or not your hypothesis was correct.

Something more   Add another $1/8$ of a teaspoon of sugar to the jug, shake it and taste it. Continue adding sugar until you can finally taste its presence. How much do you have to add before you can taste the sweetness of sugar?

Project 18

No Syrup

The concept of viscosity

Purpose You may like thick pancakes, while your friend prefers thin ones. Is it possible to control the thickness of pancakes? Let's study the viscosity of pancake batter.

Overview One of the properties of fluids is viscosity. Viscosity is the ability of a fluid to resist flowing quickly. A fluid that flows slowly is said to have a high viscosity; it is "thick." Honey, for example, has a higher viscosity than milk.

You need
- an adult
- instant pancake mix
- butter
- large spoon
- frying pan or skillet
- spatula or wide turner
- three dinner plates
- water
- use of stove
- 3 bowls
- 6 pieces of paper
- pencil or pen

Temperature can also be a factor in the viscosity of a fluid (hence the old phrase "as slow as molasses in January"). Gravy that is placed in a refrigerator overnight becomes so viscous that it turns gel-like.

Hypothesis Hypothesize that the more viscous the batter, the thicker the pancake will be when cooked.

Procedure   Use some instant pancake mix to make pancake batter. Follow the directions for adding water (or milk) and mix or stir as instructed.

Pour the batter into three bowls. Add some water to one bowl to make the batter more watery (lowering its viscosity) and stir.

To the second bowl of batter, add more of the mix powder and stir.

Do not add anything to the batter in the third bowl. Place each bowl on top of a separate piece of paper and write on each paper the contents of the bowl: "standard mix," "more water," "more powder."

With an adult standing by to help, place some butter in a skillet or frying pan, turn the stove burner on to medium heat and spread the butter to grease the pan.

Pour one large spoonful of batter from the standard-mix bowl onto a skillet and cook until golden brown. When done, place the pancake on a plate and lay a piece of paper next to it indicating "standard mix."

In the same way, pour one large spoonful of batter from the "more water" mix on the pan, and cook until golden brown. Lay the finished pancake on a plate and label it "more water." Each pancake should contain the same amount of batter. The heat applied to the pancakes will remain CONSTANT. The viscosity of the batter is the VARIABLE.

Repeat the procedure for the "more powder" batter.

When done cooking, examine each of the three pancakes. Write down your observations. Did one take longer to cook than the others?

Next, taste each one. Is there any difference in taste? Even if they all taste the same, which one is more appetizing to you, a thinner pancake or a thicker one?

If you make pancakes in the future, which will you prefer: making the batter exactly as the instructions recommend on the package, making the batter more viscous, or making it less viscous?

Results & Conclusion   Write down the results of your experiment. Come to a conclusion as to whether or not your hypothesis was correct.

Something more

1. How does the amount of time the pancake is cooked affect its thickness, if at all?
2. Does a thicker pancake absorb more syrup than a thinner pancake, making it sweeter when eaten?

Project 19

Egg Head

Measuring endothermic reactions in eggs

Purpose Boiling an egg causes a chemical reaction to take place inside the egg. This is an endothermic reaction.

Overview There is a change in energy when a chemical reaction takes place. Sometimes energy is needed to make a chemical reaction happen. A chemical reaction that absorbs energy is called an endothermic reaction. Cooking and baking are endothermic reactions. Breads and cakes rise in the oven because of the heat.

When an egg is boiled, heat is absorbed and a chemical reaction takes place inside the eggshell. You cannot see any difference between a raw egg and one that was boiled from the outside, just by looking at them. (Many people "mark" eggs they have boiled before putting them back in the refrigerator.) Yet, the heat energy absorbed has caused the egg substance inside the shell to change.

You need
- an adult
- 6 same-size eggs
- water
- cooking pot
- use of stove
- large spoon
- clock or watch
- large spoon
- 5 bowls
- paper
- pencil

Hypothesis Hypothesize that you can tell how long an egg was boiled—subjected to endothermic reaction—by making a five-egg comparison.

Procedure Place five eggs in a pot of water. Have an adult set it on a stove and bring the water to a slow boil, so as not to have the water splatter and to prevent the eggshells from cracking. Use caution when working around a stove and hot water!

Have an adult lower an egg on a large spoon carefully into the pot of boiling water. Note the time on a watch or a clock. After one minute, have the adult remove the egg. Place the egg in a bowl on a piece of paper marked "1 minute."

Repeat the procedure of boiling each egg, but boil the next one for two minutes, and the one after that for three minutes, and each additional egg for one minute longer. Lay each one in a bowl and the bowl on a piece of paper labeled with the number of minutes it sat in the boiling water. Be sure to let the eggs cool before handling them. Remember, a hot egg will not look hot. Turn off the stove when all five have been removed.

When the eggs have cooled, open each one. Keep them over their bowls, so as not to spill any contents from the eggs onto the table.

Examine each one. How has the heat affected the contents of each egg?

The temperature of boiling water is a CONSTANT, and it's assumed that all the eggs sold in a carton (marked large, extra-large, jumbo) are also CONSTANT. The amount of time each egg is boiled is the only VARIABLE.

If someone boiled another egg between one and five minutes and gave it to you, could you tell how long it had been boiled by using your five eggs as a comparison? Have a friend or family member boil an egg and, without being told how long they dipped it in boiling water, take on the role of investigator to determine about how long it was cooked, using your five eggs to make comparisons.

Results & Conclusion   Write down the results of your experiment. Come to a conclusion as to whether or not your hypothesis was correct.

Something more   How would this work with other foods, such as fried eggs or chocolate chip cookies?

Project 20

One Candle-Power

Understanding exothermic reaction

Purpose Burning causes a chemical reaction called an exothermic reaction.

Overview The previous project explained that there is a change in energy when a chemical reaction takes place. Sometimes energy must be used to make a chemical reaction happen, and sometimes energy is given off as a chemical reaction takes place. When energy is released during a chemical reaction, it is called an exothermic reaction.

You need
- an adult
- candle with straight sides (not tapered)
- gram-weight kitchen food scale
- match
- pencil
- paper
- ashtray
- butter knife
- ruler

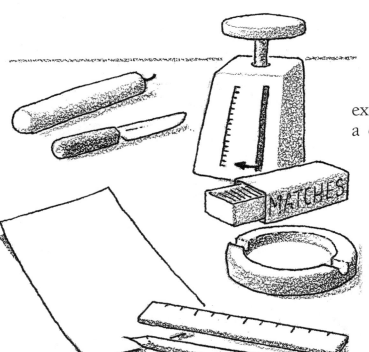

Anything that is burning is an example of exothermic reaction. When a candle is lit, the wick and wax are made to burn, causing a chemical change. This chemical reaction is invisible, in that we can't actually see the wax as it is as it is undergoing the change. It's only after the candle has been burning for a while that we see that change has actually taken place. Carbon, gas and energy in the form of heat and light are given off from a burning candle.

Hypothesis Hypothesize that if half the length of a candle is burned, a chemical reaction takes place that will cause the candle to have half its original mass (half its weight).

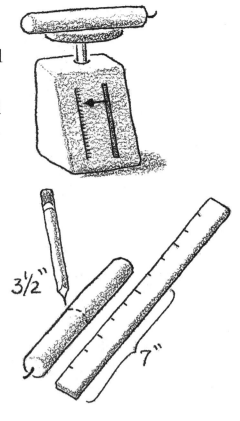

Procedure Using a gram-weight kitchen food scale, weigh a candle. Write its weight down, then use a ruler to measure the length of the candle. (Note: The candle used must have straight sides, not be tapered.) Only measure the wax; do not include the length of wick that sticks out of the candle's top. Divide the length by two to find the middle. With a pencil, make a slight mark or indentation at the point on the candle marking the middle.

Have an adult light the candle and burn it until it is half gone, and reaches the marking. Let the adult extinguish the flame, then wait a few seconds for the wick to cool. The candle is the CONSTANT. The VARIABLE is the length and mass of the candle before burning compared to after burning.

Again, weigh the candle. How much of the candle's weight was chemically changed? Into what was it changed?

Results & Conclusion Write down the results of your experiment. Come to a conclusion as to whether or not your hypothesis was correct.

Something more

1. Does the size of the candle have anything to do with the size of the flame?

2. A unit of measurement of light is "candle power," being the amount of light that is given off by one candle. But do all candles give off the same amount of light? Obviously, a bigger candle will burn longer, but is it brighter or less bright than a small candle? Can you think of a way to check this?

Project 21

Fade Not

Natural dyes and sunlight

Purpose What is the effect of sunlight on various naturally staining chemical substances, such as those that come from fruits?

Overview Your parents may have been upset when you or someone in your home spilled a certain drink or fruit juice on a good carpet. Some drinks and juices stain. Have you noticed that certain foods even stain your lips and tongue when you eat them? Could fruit or vegetable juices be used as natural dyes for clothing? If so, how do they hold up in sunlight, which often fades the synthetic dyes in carpets and upholstered chairs that are near sunny windows?

You need
- an adult
- purple grape juice
- beet juice
- blackberry juice
- old white T-shirt
- scissors
- a sunny window
- cereal bowl
- use of a sink
- several weeks' time
- old newspaper

Hypothesis
Which of the staining liquids in the experiment do you think will resist fading the most? Hypothesize that grape juice (or whichever juice you chose) will resist fading better than the others.

Procedure Take an old white T-shirt, pillowcase, or bedsheet. Check a "rag bag" if you have one, where worn or torn clothing and bedding are kept for use in cleaning or painting jobs. Cut small squares (about 3 inches/7.5 centimeters square) of white material.

Place a cereal bowl in a sink. Working in the sink will keep any juice from spilling on the floor. Pour a little blackberry juice into the bowl. Dip two white cloth squares in the blackberry juice. Lay the squares on an old piece of newspaper to dry.

Rinse the bowl with clear water. Pour in a little beet juice. Dip two white cloth squares into the beet juice and then lay them on the newspaper.

Again, rinse the bowl. Pour in a little purple grape juice. Dip two more pieces of cloth in the grape juice and lay the pieces on the newspaper to dry.

When dry, place one of each colored square in a sunny window (one blackberry, one beet and one grape juice colored squares). Place the remaining three squares in an area away from any direct sunlight. A dresser drawer or on top of the refrigerator would be good places. Can you guess which ones will fade more? Write down your guess to later check and see if you were correct.

After a week or two, compare the colors of the squares that have been in direct sunlight and also the squares that were not exposed to sunlight. Are there noticeable color changes?

The different staining juices are the VARIABLES. The sunlight in the experiment is the CONSTANT, but also in this case a VARIABLE since two pieces of cloth are stained the same—one kept in the dark (the control) and one exposed to sunlight.

Interestingly, some fluorescent-colored bathing suits come with a label attached, warning "Do not expose to direct sunlight for long periods of time!" Does the manufacturer expect people to swim only at night or indoors? Of course, too much direct sunlight isn't good for your skin either!

Results & Conclusion   Write down the results of your experiment. Come to a conclusion as to whether or not your hypothesis was correct.

Something more   Do your naturally dyed pieces of material lose their color when they are washed?

Look around your house and see if you can find discoloration caused by sunlight in the dyes in carpet and upholstered chairs and sofas. Move small furnishings a little or ask an adult to move something if the object is heavier, and look at parts of a carpet that have been covered (protected from sunlight) for many years. Is the color of the carpet the same on parts that have been largely "in the dark" as on the parts that were in direct sunlight?

Project 22
Sticky-Goo!
Emulsion, the "chem-magical" cleaner

Purpose Have you found that water alone cannot really clean an object covered with oil? Let's study the releasing property of soapy water.

Overview Remember the last time you ate some delicious fried chicken? Finger-licking good, maybe; but what happened when you tried to finish cleaning your hands by simply wiping them on a paper napkin? Did napkin shreds stick to the your fingers? Did you then try rinsing off your fingers with plain water but could still feel grease on your hands? That's when you finally gave up and grabbed the soap, right?

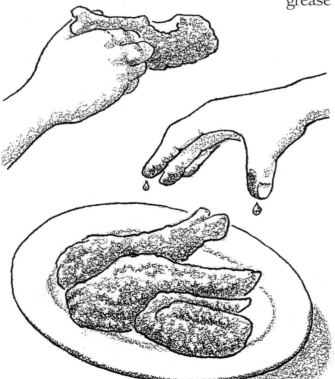

> **You need**
> * liquid dishwashing detergent
> * 2 clear drinking glasses
> * vegetable oil
> * 2 bowls
> * warm water
> * spoon

Soapy water is an emulsifier, meaning it has the ability to cut through fat and grease, turning them into tiny droplets that can be washed away. Normally, water does not mix with oil, fat, dirt and grease. The surfaces of these substances will normally resist water. Soapy water breaks through to the substances themselves so that they, with a little rubbing, are carried off into the soapy water and can be rinsed away.

Hypothesis Hypothesize that when soap is added to water its ability to remove cooking oil is improved.

Procedure Hold a clear drinking glass or mug. Tilt it a little and let some vegetable oil flow down along the inside of the glass. Do this to a second glass, also. Let the glasses dry for about a half hour.

Fill two bowls with warm water. Add liquid dish detergent to one and stir.

Dip the side of the glass that has the streak of oil into the bowl of water, then remove it. Dip the other glass in the bowl of soapy water, then take it out. Hold the glasses up to the light or in sunlight and look at the side of the glasses where the oil had flowed. Does the glass that was dipped in plain water still have vegetable oil on the side? Does the glass that was dipped in soapy water look different?

The CONSTANTS are the warm water, the surfaces of the drinking glasses and the vegetable oil. The VARIABLE is the addition of soap to one of the bowls of water.

Results & Conclusion Write down the results of your experiment. Come to a conclusion as to whether or not your hypothesis was correct.

Something more Does the temperature of the water have an effect on soapy water's ability to clean grease and oil? Fill a bowl with water and place it in a refrigerator for an hour. Fill another bowl with hot water from the kitchen faucet. (Don't make the water so hot that it might burn you.) Add an equal amount of liquid dish detergent to each bowl and stir. Pour an equal amount of vegetable oil along the inside of two glasses. Use the two batches of soapy water to clean the glasses. Does soapy hot water remove the oil easier and more thoroughly than the soapy cold water?

Project 23

Worth the Wait

Unripe fruit to sugary treat

Purpose Stores often sell fruit that doesn't taste especially good, so why keep it? Well, there's this little thing called ripening that makes all the difference.

Overview Produce that is sold by corner groceries and supermarkets is often shipped and trucked over long distances. In order for fruits and vegetables to reach those stores in good condition, they are often picked and gathered before they are ripe. This produce then ripens in transit, on the way to the grocer's bins, or soon after reaching the stores.

You need
- 1 green, unripened Bartlett, (or other) pear
- 1 yellow, slightly soft, ripened, same-type pear
- 1 green, unripened banana
- 1 yellow, ripened banana

It is important to buy and consume fruits because they contain vitamins and minerals important to a healthy diet. Mature, or ripe, fruits also contain sugar that makes them sweet and good to eat. When fruits are not fully ripe, they don't taste as sweet as they should. This is because, as a fruit ripens, a chemical process that goes on inside the fruit changes a good part of the fruit to sugar.

Unripened fruit is usually green and hard. A green banana or pear will not taste as sweet as a ripe yellow banana or pear. Unripened fruit is also sometimes hard to digest, so may cause a stomachache. On the other hand, when fruit is over-ripe, it usually turns brown. Have you ever eaten a banana that has a brown spots on it? Some people don't like the mushy texture and avoid eating brown spots in fruit, but those over-ripe spots are very sweet (brown spots can also be caused by bruising).

Hypothesis Hypothesize that a ripe banana will taste sweeter than an unripe one, and that a ripe pear will taste sweeter than an unripe one of the same type.

Procedure First, always wash off with water any produce you buy before you eat it. This will remove dirt, or any chemicals that may have been sprayed on it to protect it from insects while it was growing or during shipment.

Take a small bite of a green, hard, unripened pear (just to get a taste, you don't want that stomachache). Then take a bite of a yellow, slightly soft, ripened pear. Does one taste sweeter than the other? Which one tastes sweeter? Which one do you think contains more sugar? For fun, weigh a pear when it is not ripe, weigh it again after it ripens. Is there a difference in its weight?

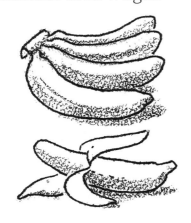

Now do the taste comparison using a green banana and a yellow banana. The taste reaction of your own taste buds to the different fruits is a CONSTANT. Also, the type of fruit remains constant (we are comparing pears to pears and bananas to bananas). The VARIABLE is the condition of the fruit, ripe or unripe.

Results & Conclusion Write down the results of your experiment. Come to a conclusion as to whether or not your hypothesis was correct.

Something more

1. How does the sweetness of ripened and unripened fruit compare to the sweetness of the same kind of fruit when it is dried? Dried banana chips, papaya, pear and pineapple are available at most supermarkets.

2. Compare the taste of an unripe, ripened and over-ripened banana. (You must eat the brown spots on the over-ripened banana. Many people do not like the thought of eating this mushy part, while some people love the sweetness of it.)

Project 24

Sweeter Sweet

Natural sugar or chemical substitute

Purpose Do people generally prefer the taste of natural sugar food products to the taste of products made with chemical sweetener substitutes?

Overview Most people love sweet-tasting foods. Even ancient peoples used sweeteners such as honey to make other foods taste better.

"Natural" table sugar is concentrated and causes health problems, including tooth decay, hyperactivity, hypertension and obesity. It is high in calories, too, so concerned people try to cut down on sugar when they diet. In response, food chemists have created sugar substitutes, to make things taste "sweet" but with fewer calories. That's why so many "low calorie" products are on the market.

"Aspartame" is one chemical often used as a sugar substitute. You may have see the word— or NutraSweet, the name it is marketed under —on low-calorie food labels. Although the ingredients making up aspartame (phenylalanine, aspartic acid and methanol) occur naturally in foods, aspartame itself does not, so there is still some controversy regarding how healthy it is for us.

You need
• an adult
• 1 box of sugar-based gelatin dessert powder (any flavor)
• 1 box of sugar-free gelatin dessert powder (same flavor and brand as sugar-based)
• kitchen measuring cup
• 10 plastic disposable spoons
• 20 paper cups
• 2 large bowls
• water
• pencils (or pens)
• 10 small notepad-sized pieces of paper
• a cooking pot
• use of a stove top burner
• use of a refrigerator
• masking tape

Aside from the health questions, how does the taste compare? Are your friends, neighbors and family members willing to drink and eat foods that use sugar substitute chemicals to benefit from the lower calories, even if they don't like the taste as much? Or, do they prefer the taste of sugar-free foods over sugar-based versions?

Hypothesis Hypothesize that more people prefer the taste of natural-sugar gelatin dessert over a sugar-substitute, aspartame, version.

Procedure At the supermarket, find a company that makes both sugar-based and sugar-free gelatin dessert products. Purchase one box of each, choosing the same flavor for both. With the help of an adult, follow the instructions on the packages and make a batch of each dessert: sugar-based and sugar-free. In this experiment, the gelatin flavor of the dessert is held CONSTANT and the sweetener is the VARIABLE.

On the bottom of a large bowl, place a piece of masking tape. Write "sugar-based" on it. Pour the sugar-based gelatin into the bowl. Place a piece of masking tape on the side and write "Sample #1" on it.

Place a piece of masking tape on the bottom of another bowl and write "sugar-free" on it. Pour the sugar-free gelatin into the bowl. Place a piece of masking tape on the side and write "Sample #2" on it. Place the two bowls in the refrigerator for cooling and hardening.

Survey 10 people by placing a spoonful of gelatin from bowl #1 into a paper cup and a spoonful of gelatin from bowl #2 into another cup. Have each person taste the gelatin from bowl #1 and #2 and write down on a piece of paper which one they liked better. Do not tell them which is which. Use a clean spoon and cups for each person you survey. Do not let anyone see the number being written down, to avoid influencing some else's opinion. Test your friends, family members, or classmates.

We are assuming that 10 people will be a large enough "sample size" to give us an approximation of what people prefer. We are using a few people to estimate how the total population may respond to the test. A sample size is when a smaller group is tested which, if large enough, will hopefully give a true picture of the large group.

Count how many people surveyed preferred gelatin sample #1 and how many preferred gelatin sample #2. Which taste did they like most?

Results & Conclusion Write down the results of your experiment. Come to a conclusion as to whether or not your hypothesis was correct.

Something more

1. Chemists use the word "sugar" to refer to the group of related carbohydrate compounds, including dextrose (corn sugar), fructose (sugar occurring naturally in fruits), lactose (milk sugar) and maltose (malt sugar). Learn more about these and other sugars. Learn about mannitol and sorbitol.

2. Test 100 people to see how accurate the results of the smaller sample group (the "10" group) was in predicting the results of the larger group.

Project 25
Chemical Tears
Overcoming an onion's natural gas

Purpose "I like onions but they make me cry." Can something be done to help the problem?

Overview Onions add their own special flavor to many of the foods we eat, from tunafish sandwiches to meat loaf. People who have backyard gardens usually grow onions, although they are not particularly high in vitamins, because of their wide use in preparing so many different dishes.

> **You need**
> • an adult
> • kitchen knife
> • 2 small same-type onions
> • large bowl or pot
> • water

The problem for the food preparer is peeling and slicing them. Onions contain a chemical in the form of an oil which easily turns into a gas whenever the onion is chopped or squeezed. The vapors given off are invisible, but affect the nose and the eyes, making tears flow and eyes burn...sometimes so much that it's hard to see.

Hypothesis It's possible to trap an onion's vapors by cutting it under water and so prevent the tearing and burning of the eyes.

Procedure First, *does* the chemical vapor of an onion carry through the air? Ask an adult to help peel, slice and squeeze a strong onion. (Be very careful working with knives. They can be very sharp.) Does the onion make your eyes burn and tear?

When your eyes are back to normal, peel, slice and squeeze another onion while it's submerged in a large bowl or pot of water. What happens? Does the water keep the vapor from escaping into the air? The onions are the CONSTANT. The VARIABLE is the environment in which the onion is cut, either in the air or in water.

Results & Conclusion Write down the results of your experiment. Come to a conclusion as to whether or not your hypothesis was correct.

Something more
1. Test several kinds of onions. Which give off the strongest vapors?
2. Do onion vapors disperse evenly throughout the air or do they *only* just rise, from chopping (waist) level to nose? How could you find out?

Project 26

Saucy Cleaner

A natural tarnish remover

Purpose Is it spaghetti's low pH that removes tarnish from copper, or is it something else?

Overview Compare a shiny new copper penny (current or recent year) to an old tarnished one. Tarnish is the results of chemical reaction over time between copper and air. Have you ever noticed a shiny spot on the tarnished copper bottom of a washed pot after a spaghetti dinner? Could spaghetti sauce be a copper cleaner?

Hypothesis Tarnish is removed by spaghetti sauce that is low pH, but low pH is not the only factor in its removing that tarnish.

> **You need**
> • spaghetti sauce
> • 2 old, tarnished copper pennies
> • 1 "new" copper penny (current or recent year)
> • cellophane tape
> • kitchen sink tap
> • lemon juice

Procedure Take an old, tarnished penny. Cover half with some tomato sauce. After a half hour, rinse the penny in water. Is the tarnish gone? Now try removing the tarnish with something other than tomato sauce, but still acidic (with low pH). We'll use lemon juice. The tarnished pennies we are testing are the CONSTANT. The VARIABLE is the substance (tomato sauce, lemon juice) applied to the coins.

Carefully place a drop of concentrated lemon juice on ½ of an old, tarnished copper penny. Cover half of the penny with cellophane or masking tape to protect it. This way we can easily make a "before-and-after" visual comparison. After about a half hour, wash the coin in water. Did the lemon juice remove the tarnish, too?

Results & Conclusion Write down the results of your experiment. Come to a conclusion as to whether or not your hypothesis was correct.

Something more Gather three similarly tarnished copper coins (compare the shades of tarnish). From three brands of prepared spaghetti sauce, place a bit of sauce onto each penny. Which brand removes the tarnish best? Read the labels on the sauces and compare their ingredients. Do any of the sauces contain acidic ingredients (for example, citric acid)?

Project 27

The Yeast Beast

Fermentation proves yeast is alive!

Purpose When yeast is used in baking,, many recipes also call for sugar as an ingredient. The yeast uses the sugar to make carbon dioxide and give the item to be baked a light and "airy" consistency. But can a sugar substitute be used instead, to activate yeast in baking and have the yeast produce carbon dioxide?

Overview For many hundreds of years, people baked bread, using yeast as an ingredient, without knowing just why it makes bread dough bubble and rise. They thought it was simply some sort of chemical reaction. It took Louis Pasteur and other scientists doing experiments in the 1850s to prove that the yeast ingredient was actually a living organism. It is this organism that causes the chemical change in bread dough.

Yeast digests sugar and starch and turns them into alcohol and carbon dioxide gas. This breaking down of sugar and starch is called fermentation. The carbon dioxide gas bubbles up through the bread dough, making the bread rise higher and become more porous (full of tiny holes). Although fermentation is also used in making alcohol, we don't taste alcohol when we eat bread with yeast, because any alcohol that is produced evaporates while the bread is being baked.

You need
• active dry yeast (available at the grocery store)
• 3 clear drinking glasses
• warm tap water
• measuring cup
• natural white sugar
• brown sugar
• sugar substitute (saccharin)

Does fermentation also take place when a sugar-substitute product is used in baking with yeast? This is an especially important question if someone wants or needs to bake sugar-free foods and is considering using a sugar substitute in a recipe.

Hypothesis More gas is released when yeast is mixed with water and sugar than if it is mixed with water and a sugar substitute.

Procedure Pour a little active dry yeast into each of three clear drinking glasses. Pour just enough to cover the bottom of each glass completely.

Add one level teaspoon of natural white sugar to one glass, one level teaspoon of brown sugar to another glass and one level teaspoon of an artificial sweetener (such as saccharin).

Measure and pour ¼ cup of warm tap water into each glass and swish the glass around, making a circular motion with your hand, to gently stir the contents. The amount of yeast and water is kept CONSTANT. The VARIABLE is the type of sweetener that is used.

Set each glass on a sheet of paper and write on the paper the type of sugar that the glass contains. When doing science experiments, it's important to label or identify each container as you do your experiments, in order to avoid confusion later.

Observe the glasses for a little while, watching for a foam of bubbles to appear, indicating the presence of carbon dioxide gas. Which one foams up the most and thus has the most response to the yeast?

Results & Conclusion Write down the results of your experiment. Come to a conclusion as to whether or not your hypothesis was correct.

Something more Experiment checking the reaction of yeast to other types of substances that contain sugar (honey or pancake syrup, for example).

Project 28

Better Bubbles

Safe and natural monster-bubble solutions

Purpose   Everybody likes to make bubbles—the bigger, the better. But is your bubble solution toxic or entirely safe?

You need
- confectioners' sugar with cornstarch
- warm water
- measuring cup
- liquid dish soap
- tablespoon
- a bottle of "bubble stuff" from the toy store
- a bubble wand (from store or homemade)
- bowl

Overview   Bubbles form in water when air is trapped. But bubbles made of water alone cannot be very large or survive in air. Something must be added to water to chemically change it so that water molecules will hold more tightly together (called surface tension).

When you buy "bubble stuff" in a toy store, an ingredient may have been added to make larger and longer-lasting bubbles (possibly glycerin) but the solution can be toxic, or poisonous if swallowed.

Hypothesis   Hypothesize that it is possible to make a monster-bubble solution that is safer, so that even little kids can enjoy making big bubbles.

Procedure   Pour ¾ cup of warm water into a bowl. Add 4 tablespoons of liquid dishwashing liquid. This liquid soap is an "emulsifier" that will help the molecules of water hold together. Stir in 2 level tablespoons of confectioners' sugar (which contains cornstarch).

Now make bubbles with the store-bought "bubble stuff," using the wand that comes with the bottle. Then, rinse off the wand and use it to make bubbles with your homemade bubble solution. The wand used to create the bubbles is the CONSTANT. The bubble solution is the VARIABLE. (You can use a pipe cleaner or some other wire bent in the shape of a wand, too, but you must use it the same way for both bubble solutions because it must remain constant for the project.)

Does your homemade bubble solution make as many bubbles and as large bubbles as the store-bought bubble liquid? If so, you have made a safe bubble toy. Of course, you still don't want to swallow your homemade soapy liquid, but it would not harm you if you did.

Results & Conclusion   Write down the results of your experiment. Come to a conclusion as to whether or not your hypothesis was correct.

Something more
1. How big can you make a bubble using your bubble solution, before the water molecules can't hold together? How long can you get a bubble to last before it pops? Why does it pop (could it be due to evaporation)? Will a bubble last longer in higher humidity (in a steamy shower, for example).
2. Is there any difference in using warm water or cold water in making your homemade bubble solution?
3. Will the kind of water matter—for example, tap water, distilled water, spring water? Does the "softness" or "hardness" of water make a difference? "Hard" water has more minerals, which usually makes it more difficult to make suds.
4. Experiment by substituting other safe ingredients. Instead of using confectioners' sugar, try honey or maple syrup as a thickening agent, but only use a very small amount.

Project 29

Onion Switch

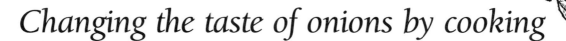

Changing the taste of onions by cooking

Purpose Onions usually have a very strong taste. Some people don't like the strong flavor, so they avoid eating onions. Can the taste of an onion be changed to make it more palatable?

Overview Heat (cooking) can affect the chemical makeup of foods and make them taste different. In onions, this chemical change makes them taste much sweeter than when the onions are raw. Test your taste buds and see if you can detect this change in sweetness, once a test-cooked onion cools down.

You need
• an adult with knife
• onion
• water
• saucepan or container
• use of stove or microwave

Hypothesis Hypothesize that cooking an onion will reduce its strong taste and give it a sweeter flavor.

Procedure Have an adult help by removing the onion ends and cutting it in half. For the CONSTANT, we need to use pieces from the same onion. Your taste buds will also remain the same. In this project, the onion is also the VARIABLE, because half will be left raw and half will be cooked.

Peel the onion. Ask an adult to cook half of the onion (sliced or not) in a little water on top of a stove or in a microwave. Once it has cooled, take out the cooked onion. Taste a bit of the raw onion and then some of the cooked onion. Compare them. Does the cooked onion taste sweeter?

Results & Conclusion Write down the results of your experiment. Come to a conclusion as to whether or not your hypothesis was correct.

Something more Make the cooked onion even tastier by making a simple white sauce to have with it. While the onion pieces are boiling in enough water to cover them, add some margarine, a sprinkle of salt, two teaspoons of cornstarch and simmer for 20 minutes. The sauce ingredients should not add sweetness, but will make the onion even more presentable, chemically, to your taste buds.

Project 30

Eaters' Digest

Dissolving foods with acids

Purpose We can't see what happens in our stomachs, or can we? We do know that some common foods (such as lemon juice and vinegar) can break down other foods, so...

Overview The organ called the stomach is very important in digestion, breaking down the foods we eat. Inside the stomach are strong acids, given off by glands, which dissolve and break down foods for energy the body needs. Do acidic foods like tea (contains tannic acid) dissolve other foods faster than plain water?

You need
• an adult
• 5 vitamin C tablets (equal strength, such as 250 mg)
• tap water
• 6 tea bags
• lemon juice
• vinegar
• 5 clear drinking glasses
• clear carbonated soda

Hypothesis Hypothesize that a vitamin C tablet will dissolve quicker in a liquid that is acidic as opposed to plain water, which has a neutral pH.

Procedure Fill five glasses with equal amounts of liquid, a quarter to half the height of the glass: tap water in one glass, vinegar in another, lemon juice in the third, and clear carbonated soda in the fourth. In the fifth, place six tea bags and hot tap water.

Let the glasses sit for an hour or until they are all at room temperature. Squeeze the tea out of the tea bags and into the glass as you remove them. The amount of liquid, tablet strength (mg), time of wait and temperature are held CONSTANT. The VARIABLE is the liquid used to try to dissolve the vitamin C tablets.

When all the liquids are at room temperature, drop a vitamin C tablet into each of the five glasses. Let the experiment sit for several hours, without disturbing the glasses. Watch the vitamin C tablet in each glass. Do the vitamin tablets dissolve faster in the acidic liquids than in the one with plain water?

Results & Conclusion Write down the results of your experiment. Come to a conclusion as to whether or not your hypothesis was correct.

Something more Would other vitamin forms (capsules, caplets) dissolve faster?

Project 31

Left Behind

It's in your water

Purpose It's possible to show that, over time, the presence of water can leave something behind from the "invisible" materials that are in it.

Overview When you look at a glass of water that you've filled from the kitchen tap, the water looks perfectly clear—like ordinary, plain water. That may be, but there are often chemicals and other substances in our tap water, or any water, that we don't see. Fluoridation of water is commonly used in fighting dental cavities. Minerals such as calcium, magnesium and iron are very often found in drinking water. Homes that have copper water pipes will sometimes have some copper in their water, too. The minerals in the water are in amounts too small to see. But, deposited and built up over time on sinks and the insides of toilet tanks, they become visible as residue.

You can get some idea of how impurities that are dissolved in a liquid can be detected by the residue (buildup of materials remaining when the liquid is gone) left behind by adding powdered chocolate to a glass of milk. Stir it with a spoon to dissolve the powder and enjoy a tasty glass of chocolate milk. When you have finished, examine the inside of the glass. Do you see a residue of chocolate on the inside of the glass, even though the milk is gone?

Hypothesis Hypothesize that, on investigation, you will be able to find residue in many places where water is often present.

Procedure Have an adult help by lifting the covering (it's heavy!) off your toilet's tank. The water inside is clear (the same water you drink from the tap), but is the inside jacket of the tank discolored and stained from mineral residue? Rub your finger along the inside. Does the chemical/mineral residue come off onto your finger? What color is it? What substance do you think is causing it?

Using your powers of observation, check the sinks around your home, school

You need
- an adult
- toilet with a tank
- sinks
- tea kettle or coffee maker
- garden hose

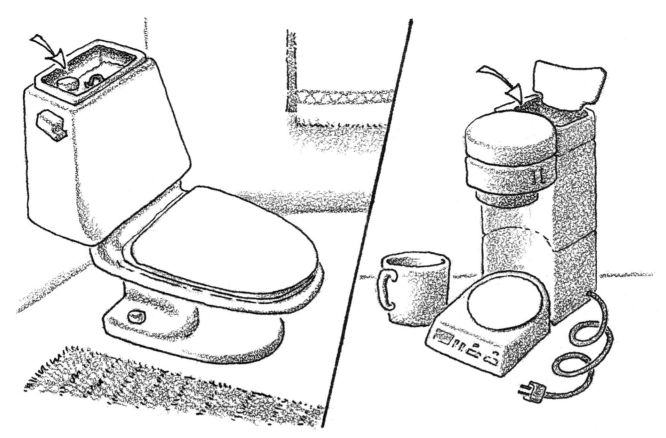

and public library to see if there are any stains or residue buildup caused by minerals in the water, and possibly a leaky faucet that causes a steady drip.

Examine the inside of a tea kettle or water tank of a coffee maker looking for the telltale stains of residue. Look for places where water drips constantly or runs past, such as the nozzle of a garden hose. The CONSTANT is the passage of water on or past the surface being examined. The VARIABLE is the item being examined.

Results & Conclusion   Write down the results of your experiment. Come to a conclusion as to whether or not your hypothesis was correct.

Something more

1. In the supermarket you can buy automatic toilet bowl cleaners which hang in your toilet tank and are activated every time you flush. Some make the water in the bowl turn blue. How do these work? Are they adding a chemical to the water?

2. Distilled water is pure water, free of minerals. It is available at supermarkets and pharmacies. Car manufacturers advise using distilled water in a car's radiator, rather than water from a home faucet. The makers of steam irons, which smooth wrinkles out of clothes, also recommend using distilled water in their irons. Why do you think these manufacturers want this especially pure water to be used in their products?

3. Can you examine the deposits taken from the inside of your toilet tank under a microscope? Can you match them to other deposits you may find around the house or school?

Project 32
Repeat, Threepeat
Exact data allows repeatable results

Purpose Accurate measurement is very important in science, and also in making cookies! Like scientists with a project, cooks need to follow a recipe *exactly* to get the kinds of result they did before: the same tasty, crunchy or chewy cookies.

Overview Sometimes a cooking or a baking recipe will call for "just a pinch" of an ingredient, or says to "season to taste." Such amounts are not precise (not "quantified," or exactly measured). In science, however, and especially in chemistry, it is important that measurements be exact and accurate so that results can be replicated (done again and again with the same result by others). We can show the importance of quantified measurement by using a recipe for baking old-fashioned sugar cookies. To do this we'll need three batches of cookies. For one batch, we'll follow the instructions using the exact measurements of the basic recipe. For the second batch, we'll use much less flour than the recipe calls for, and we'll make the third batch using far too much flour. Ask an adult to help you measure the ingredients accurately. For safety, *always* have an adult present when working around an oven or stove.

You need
• an adult
• deep bowls, spoons, mixer, measuring cups, baking tin
• sugar
• butter
• flour
• salt
• 3 eggs
• vanilla
• baking powder
• baking soda
• milk
• use of oven

Hypothesis Hypothesize that cookies from each batch will taste differently, because of a different amount of flour in each batch.

Procedure We need to mix three batches of cookie dough. All of the ingredients and their proportions will be CONSTANT, except for the flour. The amount of flour used in each batch of cookies is the VARIABLE.

Place three rows of cookies on a baking tin. Make one row from the first batch, one from the second, and one from the third. By baking samples of all the batches at the same time, we are sure that the oven temperature and baking time are variables that, for this experiment, are kept constant. This is another important point when doing a science experiment. We must hold everything constant except for the one thing we want to change, which in this case is the amount of flour used. To do this, we'll use the basic two-mix recipe below as a guide to making three cookie batches.

Old-Fashioned Sugar Cookies

In mixture #1 bowl:
- 1 cup sugar
- ½ cup butter, softened
- 1 egg
- ½ teaspoon vanilla

Mix these ingredients together.

In mixture #2 bowl:
- 2½ cups flour (2 for batch 2, 3 for batch 3)
- ½ teaspoon salt
- ½ teaspoon baking powder
- ½ teaspoon baking soda

Mix these ingredients together.

Alternately add mixture #2 and ½ cup of milk to mixture #1. Mix it until the batter is as soft it can be, then drop a full tablespoon of batter onto a baking tin. Flatten it slightly with lightly floured fingers. Drop a spoonful of cookie dough at a time onto the tin, until you have a long row of cookies. (Remember, we'll make three rows, one row of each batch of dough. Be sure to mark somehow which row is made from which mixture.) Set any extra batter in the bowl aside.

Now make another batch of cookies using the same basic recipe, except use only 2 cups of flour in mixture #2 (instead of 2½ cups as in the first batch). You can reuse the same bowls as you did for the first batch. When the dough is all mixed together, make a second row of cookies on the baking tin and set aside extra batter.

Finally, make a third batch of cookie dough, this time using 3 cups of flour for mixture #2 (instead of 2½ or 2 cups). When mixed, make a third row of cookies on the baking tin.

Have an adult help by placing the cookie tin in the oven and baking the cookies at 400 °F for 10 to 12 minutes, or until their edges are slightly brown. When done, after the cookies have cooled, taste a sample from each row—that is, one from each cookie mix. Does altering the recipe by the amount of flour have an effect on the results?

Put the extra batters together and bake more cookies to enjoy with some milk!

Results & Conclusion   Write down the results of your experiment. Come to a conclusion as to whether or not your hypothesis was correct.

Something more   Make a batch of chocolate chip cookies, but change the quantity of chocolate chips in a second batch. How has the cookie flavor changed?

Project 33

Paint by Sugars

Combining dyes

Purpose Create new food colors by combining the four common colors, usually available in packages of food coloring sets at grocery stores.

Overview Dyes are substances that combine with other substances to change their color. Dyes have been used for thousands of years. Beautifully colored dyed clothing was even found in the ancient Egyptian pyramids. Natural dyes are made from plant, animal and mineral substances. Chemists have learned to make synthetic dyes. William Perkin, a chemist, discovered a new color, "mauve," in 1856.

Think of all the things around your home that have probably been colored by dyes to make them more attractive: clothing, bath towels, bedsheets, carpeting, upholstered chairs and sofas, curtains.

Colored dyes can be combined in different amounts to make many different colors. Food coloring sets found in the supermarket usually consists of a package of four small bottles of red, green, yellow and blue coloring. These dyes can be used separately or mixed in different combinations and amounts to create a wide variety of colors.

Hypothesis Select a "mixed" color you especially like, for example, purple and hypothesize how many drops of which colors will be needed to create that color.

Procedure In a bowl, mix confectioners' sugar and water until a paste is formed. On a piece of aluminum foil, drop a dozen spoonfuls of the paste, making small mounds. Use the back side of the spoon to press a concave depression, a dent, into the top of each mound. Add different colors and amounts to each mound to create new colors. Can you predict what will happen when you add one color to another? Keep a record of how each color was formed; for example, 3 drops of red and 6 drops of yellow. The CONSTANTS are the four basic dye colors, used to form all the other colors. The VARIABLE is the amount of each color used which, when combined, helps create the new color.

Mix the colors into each mound and use the colored pasty mounds to create an artistic design or shape (heart, diamond), creature (bird shape) or to make letters on a cake. When they harden, eat them. Enjoy!

Results & Conclusion Write down the results of your experiment. Come to a conclusion as to whether or not your hypothesis was correct.

Something more

1. Create more unusual colors by combining three or even four colors in varying amounts (use a toothpick to pick up a *very* small drop of a color). Be sure to write down exactly how you got each new color, so that color can be made again by repeating the same quantities of each color.
2. Use your knowledge of coloring to create a rainbow. Be sure the colors are in the correct order as a natural rainbow.
3. Select simple color art from a magazine or book and try matching the colors to use as "paint" to reproduce the picture.

Project 34

Colorful Disguise

Smell and taste: team players

Purpose How important is the sight of a food in its identification, compared to smell and taste?

Overview Our senses of smell and taste are chemical processes that our bodies use as a team to help us evaluate foods. But do you think it is easy to identify a food from taste only, or in combination with smell, without the aid of the sense of sight?

To test this, we want to prepare pieces of several fruits and vegetables for various friends and others to sample a taste. And, since they may be able to identify even a small piece of fruit or vegetable by sight (and we'd rather not subject them to being blindfolded), we will disguise each food sample so it cannot easily be identified.

To carry out the experiment, we'll need to use fruits and vegetables with similar textures. Then we'll cut the pieces into very small cubes and change the normal "look" of the food with food coloring, so its color will not be a help in guessing a food's identity.

You need
- an adult
- several friends
- apple
- pear
- cucumber or squash
- cantaloupe or other melon
- knife
- 4 bowls or containers
- aluminum foil
- blue food coloring
- eye-dropper
- paper and pencil

Hypothesis Your friends will make more incorrect (or correct) guesses than correct (or incorrect) guesses based on taste alone…or based on both taste and smell.

Procedure Have an adult help you cut the *fleshy* part of an apple, a pear, a melon such as a cantaloupe or honeydew, and a cucumber into a number of small cubes. Be sure not to include any seeds or skins, which might be a help in identifying the food.

Place apple pieces in one bowl, melon in another, pear in a third and cucumber in a fourth bowl. Write the name of each test fruit or vegetable onto a piece of masking tape and stick it onto the bottom of the proper bowl of test samples.

Now take a single piece of each fruit or vegetable and place it in a small section of aluminum foil and close it up loosely. Place it alongside the bowl of fruit samples. Disguise the remaining cubes of food in the bowl with *blue* food coloring (except for berries, blue is not a common fruit or vegetable coloring).

Place the sampling bowls at least a few feet apart and, one by one, have a few of your friends approach a bowl. While holding their nose tightly, have them take a cube of food, taste it and guess what they think it is…*by taste alone*. Then let them sniff the bowl of colored fruit pieces, thereby adding the sense of smell, and allow them to change their taste-only guess if they wish to. Once each friend finishes the test, let him or her see the normal-colored fruit pieces that you placed in each foil packet. Are your friends now able to recognize the fruit? Keep track of all their guesses. You can use the information to make up a chart for your project display.

The senses used by each individual taking the test and the fruits used remain CONSTANT. The color of the fruits are the VARIABLE from their natural color. Tally how many guesses were right after tasting and after smelling (and seeing with normal coloring) and how many were wrong.

Results & Conclusion   Write down the results of your experiment. Come to a conclusion as to whether or not your hypothesis was correct.

Something more
1. Do the above experiment, first testing five kids your age and then five adults. Do you think adults will have more correct guesses than your friends?
2. Select other fruits and vegetables that have similarly fleshy parts so they could be used in this type of taste test. How about squash and tomato? What about the strength (sweet, sour, bitterness) of the flavors?
3. In addition to fruits and vegetables, do a similar experiment using cubes of lunch meat, for example, bologna and turkey breast, or different cheeses.

Project 35

You've Changed!

Identifying chemical and physical changes

Purpose Understanding the difference between a physical change and a chemical change.

Overview Some changes which take place in substances are "physical changes" and some are "chemical changes." What is the difference?

When a chemical change takes place, the substance often takes on new properties. Glass is made from sand and limestone, but has properties unlike either sand or limestone. Carbon, hydrogen and oxygen can be combined to form table sugar, a compound that is nothing like the elements that make it up. Hydrogen and oxygen by themselves burn, but when two atoms of hydrogen combine with one atom of oxygen it forms a molecule of water, which not only doesn't burn, but can be used to put out fires!

It is often difficult or impossible to "undo" the results of a chemical reaction. However, a physical change can usually be reversed.

For example, heat may cause a chemical change. Compare a slice of bread to one that has been toasted. The heat has caused a chemical change in the bread, and we cannot restore the bread to the way it was before it was toasted. A log burning in a fireplace is having its chemical composition changed to carbon, heat, light, sound and gases. It would be impossible to combine carbon, gases and remove heat to restore the log to its former state.

Water can be changed by temperature to take the form of a gas, a liquid, or a solid (ice). This is not a chemical change; it is a physical change. Ice can easily be turned back into a liquid, and the liquid retains all of the same properties it had when it was previously a liquid. This is a case where heat causes a physical change but not a chemical change.

You need
- drinking glasses
- water
- ice cubes
- 2 slices of bread
- use of a toaster
- pepper
- fruit (for fruit salad)
- fresh milk
- sour milk
- unbaked cookie dough
- baked cookies

Hypothesis By gathering together some common everyday materials, it is possible to clarify and display the results of three physical changes and three chemical changes.

Procedure Set up the following examples of change and explain the differences:

Physical change:
#1. a glass of water and ice cubes
#2. a glass of plain water and a mixture of water and black pepper (pepper does not combine with water, and can be easily removed)
#3. cut-up fruits and a fruit salad (even though fruit pieces are mixed together, you can still pull out individual slices to separate them again)

Chemical change:
#1. a slice of bread and a slice of toasted bread
#2. unbaked cookie dough and a baked cookie
#3. fresh milk and sour milk

The foods you start with, before any changes are made to them, are the CONSTANT.

The physical VARIABLE with water and water containing pepper is the addition of pepper; with water and ice cubes is temperature; with cut-up fruit and fruit salad is the mixing.

The chemical VARIABLE with bread and toasted bread and with unbaked and baked cookie dough is the addition of heat; with fresh and sour milk is the souring.

Results & Conclusion Write down the results of your experiment. Come to a conclusion as to whether or not your hypothesis was correct.

Something more
1. Can you name some physical changes that, at first, appear to be chemical changes. For example, adding powdered drink mix to water. It is physical, because the water can be separated from the mix by evaporation (leaving the mix behind). Baking cookies is a chemical change. Breaking the finished cookie in half to share with a friend is a physical change.
2. If newspaper is placed in a sunny window for several days, it changes color. Is that a physical or chemical change? Can it be easily reversed?
3. Is rotting fruit a chemical or a physical change?

Project 36

Scent in a Cube
Releasing fragrance with heat

Purpose You know that flowers outside give off fragrances and will do so in your home, if you bring them inside. But how can you make something in your home give off more of its scent?

Overview Smell is a chemical process that takes place as tiny invisible molecules leave an object and travel through the air to reach our nose, where a chemical solution and nerve cells line the inside of the nose to detect the smell.

> **You need**
> • an adult
> • bar of soap with a fragrance
> • knife
> • microwavable dish
> • use of a microwave oven

Smells can remind us of special times and events. The smell of cedar may make you think of a cedar chest someone in your family uses to store clothing. If you decorate a live tree at Christmas time, you may get the feeling of that season when you smell that particular kind of tree. Think about what odors remind you of a happy time at home during a holiday, or a visit to grandma's house. Many people like the smell of peppermint, apple, pine and cinnamon. They buy candles that are scented, which give off their aroma when lit. They buy incense burners to spread an aroma throughout their room. There are small potpourri pots where water and pieces of fragrance are heated with a small candle underneath.

Heat can cause a material to release molecules into the air and be diffused (going from an area of more concentration to an area of lesser concentration). Then we can detect the airborne molecules with our nose. That is why a scented candle can be in a room, but you won't smell it until it is lit, and the potpourri pot does not release its scent until it is warmed.

Hypothesis Hypothesize that heat will cause the fragrance in a perfumed soap to be released and fill the air in a room with an aroma.

Procedure Have an adult carefully cut a small cube from a bar of soap that is perfumed or has a fragrance. Notice that you probably do not notice the scent very much unless you place the soap fairly close to your nose. The soap is CONSTANT. The VARIABLE is the heat that is applied to the soap.

Place the soap on a microwavable dish and place it in a microwave oven. Heat it for several seconds. Microwave ovens have different powers, so you may have to experiment with the amount of time. Start with about five seconds.

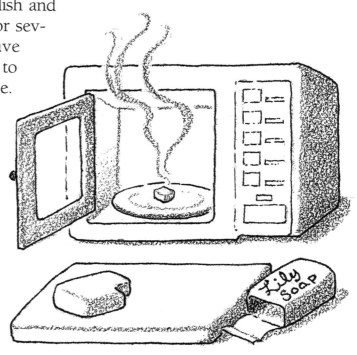

Open the door of the microwave, but *don't touch the soap*; it may not *look* hot to you, but it might still be hot enough to burn. After a few minutes, walk around the room and sniff the air. Can you detect the soap's smell in all areas of the room? How about in the next room?

Results & Conclusion Write down the results of your experiment. Come to a conclusion as to whether or not your hypothesis was correct.

Something more
1. Can the same piece of soap be reheated again and again to release even more fragrance?
2. Purchase two identical car fresheners, the small decorative fresheners made to hang from the rearview mirror. Put one in a sealable plastic bag and place it in a refrigerator freezer. Place the other in a sunny window. Later, remove the one from the refrigerator and open the bag. Is its smell as strong as the freshener in the sunny window? If the freshener in the sunny window has a stronger smell, does this mean that car fresheners give off more scent in the summertime than they do in winter?

Project 37

Staying on Top

Reduce a soap's density...and it floats!

Purpose Soap normally sinks—but can it be changed in some way so it will float in water?

Overview The "density" of a material refers to how closely packed together the matter is that makes it up. The density of an object determines its weight, or mass, but not its size. A piece of metal that is exactly the same size as a piece of cork will be denser than the cork. Objects that are less dense than water will be supported by the water and so will float.

Look at a sponge used for cleaning and compare it to a block of wood the same size. The sponge is less dense; it contains less material than the wood, yet it is the same size. The sponge weighs less than the wood.

One feature of a popular brand of soap is that it floats. That's because it's less dense than water. Is it possible to decrease the density of a soap that normally doesn't float, so it will? One way to make a substance less dense is to expand its size and add air into it, making it less compact. We will use heat to expand the soap.

Hypothesis Hypothesize that you can change the shape and density of a piece of soap but its weight will not change.

Procedure Lay a pencil on a flat table. The pencil should have flat surfaces on it, not round. Set a ruler across the pencil, at about the middle of the ruler, so that it looks like a seesaw. Use adhesive tape to fix a nickel near each end of the ruler.

Have an adult cut two small chunks out of a bar of soap. Place one chunk in a small bowl filled with water. Be sure the soap sinks. This ensures that we are using soap that will normally sink when placed in water. Set the other chunk on one of

> **You need**
> • an adult
> • bar of soap that does not float in water
> • knife
> • 2 nickels
> • several pennies
> • several paper clips
> • ruler
> • adhesive tape
> • pencil with flat sides (not round)
> • paper plate
> • cereal bowl filled with water
> • use of microwave oven

the nickels at the end of the ruler. Lay pennies and paper clips on the other end of the ruler until the ruler balances as best as possible on the pencil.

Lift the chunk of soap off the ruler, being careful not to disturb the pennies and paper clips. Lay the soap on a paper plate and place it in a microwave oven. Because microwave ovens differ in the amount of power they have, you will have to experiment with time. Start by running the oven for 10 seconds. Watch the soap. We are watching for it to expand and look more like whipped cream than a solid chunk. Try running the oven for another 5 seconds if you haven't observed much change in the soap.

When the soap seems to have expanded, foaming up like whipped cream, remove the plate from the oven, but *don't touch* the soap for a few minutes until it cools.

Carefully lay the puffed-out soap back on top of the nickel on the ruler. The balance scale system, used to weigh the soap before and after being exposed to the microwave oven, is the CONSTANT. The VARIABLE is the addition of heat from a microwave being applied to the piece of soap.

We are using the nickel because now the soap has changed to a bigger shape and we want to be sure we place the soap at the same point on the ruler that it was before. The soap should rest completely on the nickel and not touch the ruler.

Does the soap still balance? We increased the "volume" or size of the soap and decreased its density (the material is now more spread out), but we haven't changed its weight significantly. Most all of the material that was present before it was heated is still there, so it weighs the same. The balance-scale system used to weigh the soap before and after being exposed to the microwave oven is CONSTANT. The VARIABLE is the heat from a microwave which is applied to the piece of soap.

Place the puffed soap in the bowl of water. Have we reduced the density enough so that it now floats?

Results & Conclusion Write down the results of your experiment. Come to a conclusion as to whether or not your hypothesis was correct.

Something more
1. Do you think soap that has been expanded and made less dense will be used up more quickly in the shower? The surface area of the expanded soap is greater, so more of it will be exposed to the water and the washcloth when you're washing.
2. Take a lump of clay and place it in water. It will sink. Mold it into the shape of a row boat and place it in the water again. Does the clay still sink or does it now float?

Project 38
Basic Building Blocks
Getting to know the Periodic Table

Purpose There are natural rules on how elements will or will not combine with each other.

Overview Everything in the world is made up of basic "elements." In chemistry, an "element" is matter than cannot be separated into simpler parts by either chemical or physical means.

Some things are made of two or more elements that have combined. Metals, wood, plants, bodily tissues and even the air we breathe are combinations of elements.

Elements are made up of tiny, invisible particles called atoms. Atoms are made up of even smaller parts, and some atoms have more parts than others. One atom part is called a "proton." Every element has been given a number, called its "atomic number," which is the number of protons one atom of that element contains.

Chemists learned that the elements could be arranged, based on their atomic number, in rows and columns to form a helpful table. This table is called the Periodic Table because it displays a regular pattern of properties among the elements.

You need
• several different sets of young children's building toys (for example, Lego, Megablocks, Tinker Toys, Lincoln Logs, Erector Set and traditional wooden blocks)

28 **Ni** Nickel 58.71	29 **Cu** Copper 63.54	30 **Zn** Zinc 65.37
46 **Pd** Palladium 106.4	47 **Ag** Silver 107.87	48 **Cd** Cadmium 112.40

Atomic Number

Symbol for the Element

Name of the Element

Average Atomic Mass

IRON

COPPER

SILVER

Some elements have similar properties and features, and we say these elements make up a "family."

Chemists have given elements one or more letter symbols to represent their name: Zn for zinc, Cu for copper, Ag for silver, etc. The first letter is always capitalized and, if there are additional letters, they are written in lower-case, or non-capped letters. The symbols are used on the periodic table, and are also used when equations are written, showing the combining of elements and their results.

Hypothesis   Hypothesize that toy construction pieces will easily fit together if they are from the same "family" or type of toy, but pieces from different sets will not work well together.

Procedure   Using different sets of children's building toys, show how the building pieces from the same "family" fit together, but they do not fit together with pieces from other building toys. The construction pieces within a given set are CONSTANT. The construction pieces from different sets when tried to be combined are VARIABLE.

This is similar to elements on the period table; some elements combine more easily. In fact, when sodium combines with water it explodes!

Results & Conclusion   Write down the results of your researches and come to a conclusion as to whether or not your hypothesis was correct.

Something more

1. Which element do you think is the most abundant on Earth? Research "Periodic Table" under "Elements" in an encyclopedia volume or computer CD-ROM. Look on the Internet for the very latest information, because new elements, mostly synthetic radioactives, are still being discovered. (Recently, 109 Unnileanium and 110 Unununium were created in laboratories—but lasted for only a fraction of a second).
2. Zn is the symbol for zinc. O is the symbol for oxygen. You can easily see how these symbols were chosen to represent their elements. But the symbol for iron is Fe; sodium is Na; potassium is K. Research how these symbols were derived.

Project 39

Stressed Out

The effects of weathering on elasticity

Purpose Rubber bands are elastic…until something happens. Let's examine how stress and weather conditions affect elastic bands.

Overview Signs of deterioration in a rubber band are discoloring, cracking and splitting, and the loss of elasticity (it doesn't return completely to its original shape). This is what happens when you see a rubber band that has been left outside for even a few days. Yet, rubber bands left in a drawer in your home can stay there, sometimes for years, without showing signs of deterioration.

What is it about the outdoors that might affect the rubber material? Perhaps ozone or other gases in the air attack rubber. There may be acids in rain. Sunlight contains ultraviolet and infrared rays which may alter rubber material. Temperature and humidity changes may also be a factor.

Hypothesis Hypothesize that a rubber band that is stressed (stretched) and exposed to the outside elements will show definite signs of deterioration within a few days, while one under the same stress but kept indoors, will show little or no deterioration in that short time.

Procedure In addition to comparing two stressed rubber bands, one indoors and one outdoors, let's also try to narrow down the possible cause of deterioration. The rubber bands are the CONSTANT. The stretching and exposure to outdoor elements are the VARIABLES.

Bend the metal opener tab on a soda can upward so that, while still attached to the can, the tab is at a 90-degree angle to the can top. Push a small rubber band halfway through the hole in the tab.

> **You need**
> - 3 equal-size small rubber bands
> - 3 paper clips
> - 3 empty soda cans (with pull tabs)
> - water
> - magnifying glass
> - index card
> - hanging area outside
> - hanging area inside

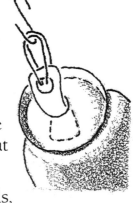

Bend a paper clip to form an "S"-shaped hook and hang the two loop ends of the rubber band onto one paper-clip hook. Bend the hook closed to keep the rubber band from slipping out. In the same way, put rubber bands and hooks on two more cans.

Fill all three cans half-full of water. Using the other end of the paper-clip hooks, hang two cans outdoors on a clothesline that is in full sunlight. Find an out-of-the-way spot indoors to hang the third can. You can hang it on a bedroom door jam (the molding around the door). Be sure the indoor can is not in direct sunlight, as it would be if you hung it on a window curtain rod.

You can add more water or remove some to make the rubber bands you have stretch, but not stretched to their maximum.

Let the cans hang from their stretched rubber bands for five to seven days. If rain is coming, move one of the two outdoor cans indoors and hang it from the door jam. When the rain stops, take the can back outside and hang it on the clothesline again. Be sure to mark this can so you can identify it as being the one that is usually outdoors but is not exposed to rain.

Now you have three stressed rubber bands: one kept indoors away from the elements of weather and sunlight; one outdoors that is fully exposed to sunlight, air, temperature changes and rain; and one that is exposed to sunlight, temperature changes and air, but not rain.

Check your rubber bands daily. One or both of the outdoor rubber bands may deteriorate so much as to break before a week has passed. At that time, end your experiment and examine all three rubber bands.

Examine them by looking at each one under a magnifying glass. Has there been a change in color? Do you see cracks or splits developing? Cracks can also be detected by holding a rubber band in the stretched position and running the edge of an index card up and down the length of it. You will hear a noise if cracks have developed.

Check the elasticity of the rubber bands. Do they snap back to their original shape when stretched?

Results & Conclusion   Write down the results of your experiment. Come to a conclusion as to whether or not your hypothesis was correct.

Something more

1. Try this experiment using rubber bands of different sizes, thicknesses and colors.
2. Try this experiment using other elastic materials; for example, strips of inner tube or party balloons.

Project 40

Heavy Gas, Man
Releasing trapped gas to extinguish flame

Purpose To learn about an important characteristic of carbon dioxide, that it is heavier than air—and how that characteristic can be used.

Overview Does the chemical term "sodium bicarbonate" sound familiar to you? Actually, you probably have a box of it in your home. Maybe you will recognize it more by its common name, "baking soda."

Baking soda is a white powder that has many uses. In the kitchen it is often called for in baking recipes. In the bathroom, it is used as a tooth cleaner...for brushing teeth. Added to a laundry load, it enhances the action of liquid chlorine bleach, to make clothes whiter. When placed in the refrigerator, it absorbs food odors. As an antacid, it helps relieve heartburn and sour stomach. It can even be used in a bowl of warm water to soothe aching feet. Sodium bicarbonate is truly a useful household chemical.

Baking soda can also be used in the kitchen for putting out small fires; for example, a grease fire in a frying pan. When baking soda is thrown on a fire, the powder helps cover whatever is fueling the fire and cuts it off, like a blanket, from exposure to air. But its real fire-fighting ability comes from its release of carbon dioxide gas, caused by the heat of the fire. Carbon dioxide gas actually puts out fires.

Carbon dioxide gas can also be released from baking soda by mixing the soda with vinegar. Since carbon dioxide gas is also heavier than air, it stays near the ground if free or, if in a container, will stay in the bottom of it until it's released.

Hypothesis Hypothesize that you can put out the flame of a candle by releasing carbon dioxide gas from baking soda and "pouring it" onto the flame.

Procedure Set a votive candle in a short glass or coffee mug. Have an adult light the candle.

> **You need**
> • an adult
> • matches
> • votive candle
> • a short drinking glass or mug
> • vinegar
> • baking soda
> • coffee can
> • tablespoon measure

Take an empty coffee can filled only with air. Carefully, tilt the can over the glass containing the candle, as if you are "pouring" air into the glass. (Always be alert and careful working around open flame or anything hot.) Observe that there is no change in the lit candle when you "pour" the air.

Next, scoop two tablespoons of baking soda and dump them into the empty coffee can. Pour three tablespoons of vinegar into a small glass or container. Pour the vinegar quickly, all at once, into the coffee can containing the baking soda. A violent reaction will take place and carbon dioxide gas will be released, causing bubbles to foam up. When the fizzing has settled down after two or three seconds, quickly tilt the coffee can and pour the "invisible" carbon dioxide gas in the can onto the lit candle. Be careful not to tilt the can so much that the baking soda mixture itself spills out and makes a mess. Does the flame on the candle go out?

The flame and the candle are the CONSTANTS. The VARIABLE is the addition of carbon dioxide gas.

Although the carbon dioxide gas that is poured out can't be seen, you can detect its presence by its effect on the lit candle.

Results & Conclusion   Write down the results of your experiment. Come to a conclusion as to whether or not your hypothesis was correct.

Something more   Is there enough carbon dioxide generated to put the candle out even if it is *not* sitting in a small cup? Can you possibly measure the amount of a gas you cannot see?

Project 41

Have a Taste, Bud

Sugar sweetness a matter of chemistry

Purpose We experience the sense of taste when we eat or otherwise put things in our mouths. What do we taste and why do we taste it? Let's find out.

Overview The sense of taste is a chemical action that takes place on our tongues. Test that that taste is a chemical process by laying a dry cornflake on your tongue. It won't have any taste at all until your saliva begins dissolving it. Do the same with a dry cracker.

Because food must be dissolved before it can be tasted is proof that taste is a chemical process. It is only possible for us to taste foods that are in a liquid state. If they're not, the saliva in our mouth dissolves the food, turning it into a liquid.

Small organs, called "taste buds," on our tongues then evaluate the dissolved food and give us the sensation of taste. Four sets of taste buds are used to detect the sweet, sour, salty and bitter taste groups. As shown, these four kinds of taste buds are located at different areas on top of the tongue.

You can easily test this; open your mouth wide and briefly rub a piece of peppermint stick against the back part of your tongue, being careful not to touch the front part. Don't place the candy too far back on your tongue or it might make you gag. After a brief

> **You need**
> • corn flakes
> • crackers
> • peppermint stick hard candy
> • piece of licorice
> • cherry lollipop
> • grape lollipop
> • lemon lollipop
> • glass of water

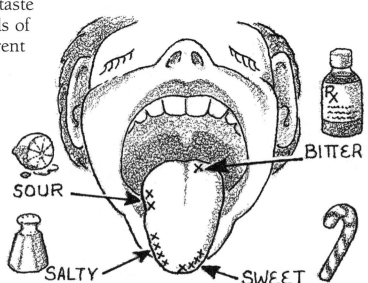

74

rubbing , notice any taste in your mouth. Now rub the peppermint on the front area of your tongue. Can you taste the sweetness of the candy better?

Hypothesis Hypothesize that the organs that cause you to be able to taste and isolate flavors are grouped on top of the tongue.

Procedure Place a hard candy peppermint stick under your tongue and a small piece of licorice on top of your tongue. Wait a few moments for your saliva to dissolve some of the candies. Which candy do you taste?

Take a sip of water to clear the taste from your mouth (official tasters call it "clearing the palate"). Now reverse the candies, placing a licorice piece under your tongue and touching the peppermint stick to its top. Which candy do you taste now?

Experiment further by placing various flavors of lollipop under your tongue and onto areas of its surface; try cherry, grape, lemon, lime and other flavors that you know and are easy to identify. Your tongue with its taste buds is the CONSTANT. It's the different *areas* of the tongue undergoing testing that are the VARIABLES, as are the different lollipop flavors.

Results & Conclusion Write down the results of your experiment. Come to a conclusion as to whether or not your hypothesis was correct.

Something more Prepare small pieces of fruit: orange, apple, grape, peach, and others. Have friends close their eyes while you lay a piece of fruit on their tongues. Can they identify the fruit? Can they tell the difference between sweet, sour, salty and bitter?

Project 42

Settle Up

Oil and water don't mix…usually

Purpose To determine if an oil spill would clean up quicker in freshwater than in saltwater.

Overview When huge ships carrying oil (oil tankers) have an accident that causes a breach (a hole) in their hull, thousands of gallons of oil can leak into the water. Oil spills are terrible environmental problems. The oil pollutes the water and often harms fish and wildlife.

You may have heard the old saying "Oil and water don't mix." It is true that oil, including cooking oil found in your kitchen, does not mix easily with water. It has a tendency to float on top of water. Have you ever watched someone cooking spaghetti and seen them add a little vegetable oil to the pot of boiling water? Did you notice that the oil stayed on top of the water?

The fact that oil floats on water certainly helps environmental crews who are assigned the task of cleaning up oil spills from oil tankers. In the open sea, it would be nearly impossible to contain oil if it immediately mixed with water and was carried down to all depths by currents, as well as spreading out from the ship.

Does oil float better in saltwater than freshwater? If so, then would an oil spill in saltwater be easier to clean up than one in freshwater? If the oil and water are slightly mixed, as they would be by waves in the ocean, does the oil settle up quicker in one type of water than the other? That would make oil cleanup quicker, although not necessarily easier.

Hypothesis Form a hypothesis as to whether you think oil mixed with water settles up (floats) quicker in saltwater or freshwater. Or, you hypothesize that there is no noticeable difference.

You need
• 2 clear jars with screw-top lids
• water
• vegetable oil
• salt
• tablespoon measure
• kitchen measuring cup
• spoon
• clock or watch
• masking tape
• pen or pencil

Procedure Gather two clear jars with lids that screw on tight. A pickle, mayonnaise, relish or jelly jar make good choices. The two jars must be identical in size.

Pour ¾ cup of water into one jar. Pour another ¾ cup of water into the second jar. To the second jar add 4 tablespoons of salt. Stir.

Stick a piece of masking tape on each jar and label which one is freshwater and which one is saltwater, by writing on the tape. Although it is not actual ocean brine, the saltwater solution will approximate the saltwater found in the sea.

Pour ¼ cup of vegetable oil into each jar. Screw the lids on the jars. Shake each jar lightly several times (be sure to shake each jar the same number of times). This shaking is to simulate the action of the waves in the ocean. The oil in this project is a CONSTANT. The water is VARIABLE, comparing both fresh- and saltwater.

Make a note of the time. Set the jars on a table and don't disturb them. Observe the jars, waiting for the oil and water to settle out.

Does the oil in one jar settle out more quickly than in the other? If so, that would make an oil spill in that type of water quicker to clean up, although not necessarily easier. The quicker an oil spill can be cleaned up, the less chance it has to have a hazardous effect on the environment.

Results & Conclusion Write down the results of your experiment. Come to a conclusion as to whether or not your hypothesis was correct.

Something more Do you live near an ocean or a lake whose water is salty? Repeat the above experiment, but instead of using homemade saltwater, use actual salt water from the saltwater body near you. Is there any difference between the results of your homemade saltwater and actual brine? If not, then the homemade saltwater was a good representation of actual sea water.

Is there anything that can be added to water—fresh or sea water—to aid in the picking up of oil?

Project 43

Building Blocks

Growing natural crystal structures

Purpose Certain substances just naturally take flat-sided crystalline shapes. Here's how to watch, as you "grow" your own crystals.

Overview Everything is made up of small particles called atoms and molecules. In some solid substances, these atoms and molecules are arranged together to make three-dimensional patterns, which are repeated over and over until they are big enough for us to see with a microscope or a magnifying glass. These substances are called "crystals." Crystals have shapes that are characterized by their smooth, flat surfaces with sharp edges. Crystal-shaped substances include sugar, table salt, gold, silver, topaz, quartz and copper sulfate.

Although non-living things do not grow, the molecules of crystals can pile together to "grow" bigger in size. When enough sugar is dissolved into water, sugar crystals will build up or "grow" on a piece of thread or string that is left in the solution until a clump big enough to see with the unaided eye appears.

Examine a few grains of sugar under a microscope. If you do not have a microscope, you can use a magnifying glass that has a high magnification. Observe that the tiny grains of sugar have a cube- or block-like shape. This is one kind of crystal shape.

Examine a few grains of table salt under a microscope or a magnifying glass of high magnification. Observe that salt, too, has a cube-like shape and therefore i t is also called a crystal.

Hypothesis Hypothesize that, since you have observed salt to be a crystal, it too can be made to accumulate (build up) and "grow" a large crystal object.

You need
- an adult
- salt
- sugar
- 2 short drinking glasses
- thin string or thread
- spoon
- hot water from the tap
- 2 pencils
- magnifying glass (microscope preferable)

Procedure   Fill a short drinking glass with hot water from the tap. Be careful not to burn yourself! Add a spoonful of sugar to the water and stir. Continue to add one spoonful at a time and stir until no more sugar can be dissolved in the water. You can tell when this happens, as sugar will begin to build up at the bottom of the glass and will not dissolve, no matter how long you stir. When a solution is holding as much of a substance as it can, it is called a "saturated solution." A "solution" is a solvent (the material that you use to dissolve) that contains a solute (the material that gets dissolved).

Tie a piece of thread or thin string onto a pencil at its center. Lay the pencil on top of the glass of sugar water and let the string hang down into the water. Set the glass in an out-of-the-way place, where it will not be bumped or moved. Wait two to three days. Then observe the buildup of sugar crystals on the string. We are "growing" a big crystal from many small crystals.

Fill another short drinking glass with hot water from the tap. Use caution handling hot water so as not to burn yourself. Stir in a spoonful of table salt. Continue to add salt and stir until the solution has become saturated (no more salt can be dissolved and excess salt can be seen at the bottom of the glass). Tie a piece of thread or thin string onto the center of a pencil. Lay the pencil on top of the glass and let the string hang down into the solution.

The water and string are CONSTANT. The solute (the material being dissolved) is the VARIABLE (sugar and salt). After two or three days, examine the string. Have crystals of salt begun to build up on the string? Was your hypothesis correct?

Results & Conclusion   Write down the results of your experiments and come to a conclusion as to whether or not your hypothesis was correct.

Something more

1. Can you build your crystal objects even bigger by adding more sugar and salt to the solutions and waiting a few more days? Do not heat the water again, because you don't want to dissolve the crystals that have already formed on the string. You want to add to them.

2. Ice can form crystal structures, too. On a morning when frost makes designs on your house windows or car windshield, use a magnifying glass of high magnification to examine the frost for evidence of crystal shapes.

3. Honey can crystallize and turn into a solid; but can it be restored to a liquid form by warming it?

Project 44

Cool Clothes

Testing for fabrics that "breathe"

Purpose Sometimes you need to dress to keep warm, other times you want to wear clothing that "breathes" to help you stay cooler. How can we test fabrics for their ability to allow the body to cool itself in summer through evaporation?

Overview Clothes...everybody wears them. Different types of clothing are worn for different seasons, weather and climates. Years ago, people made clothes from whatever they found in nature. From animals, they got fur, leather and wool. From plants, they used grasses, weaved straw and grew cotton to make fabric.

Now chemists have developed new materials for clothing. Some of these "synthetics" have greater benefits than clothing made from plants and animals. Rayon, for example, is a synthetic fabric that is strong, yet soft. It is easy to dye and the colors don't fade. In 1939, the DuPont Company began marketing a synthetic fiber called nylon, which quickly became the standard for women's stockings. Nylon was originally developed for its strength and its light weight, perfect for making parachutes. Surprisingly, many of the new synthetic materials are made from *petro*chemicals; in order words, they are are *oil-based* products.

Which types of clothing material are best for keeping warm in winter? Which are best for keeping you cool in summer? Articles of clothing made from polyester fibers are said to allow the vapor of perspiration to pass through easily, keeping the person who wears a polyester shirt cooler than with some other types of material. Perspiration causes evaporation, which is a cooling process.

Hypothesis A piece of polyester shirt fabric covering a bowl of water will allow more of that water to evaporate than will other popular shirt materials.

> **You need**
> - 3 clear wide-mouth jars (or clear bowls)
> - 2 rubber bands
> - 2.5 ounce baby-food jar (or similar small cup)
> - 3 7-ounce disposable plastic or paper cups (or similar small cups)
> - cotton shirt
> - polyester shirt
> - water
> - a week's time

Procedure Fill three clear wide-mouth jars with an equal amount of water. In order to accurately measure an amount of water for each, fill a tiny jar (for example, a 2.5 ounce baby-food jar) with water until it overflows. Then carefully, without spilling any water, pour the complete contents into one of the jars. Repeat this for the other two jars.

Look at the labels on the shirts in your closet or in the closet of others in your home. Collect a shirt that is made of polyester and one made of cotton.

Lay a single layer of the polyester clothing over one of the water-filled jars. Stretch a rubber band around the jar to secure it. Lay a single layer of the cotton clothing over one of the water-filled jars. Stretch a rubber band around the jar to secure it.

Leave one jar uncovered. Set the jars in an out-of-the-way place where they will not be disturbed. Let them sit for a week.

The CONSTANT is the amount of water, the size of the jars (the opening at the top where evaporation takes place) and the period of time. The VARIABLE is the type of material covering the jars, affecting evaporation of the water in the jar.

After one week, remove the shirts from the jars. Measure the amount of water left in each of the three jars and compare. Did the uncovered jar have the most evaporation? Did the cotton-covered jar have the least? If you have trouble comparing the amounts of water left, pour the contents of each into three smaller/narrower containers (such as disposable plastic or paper cups). Then the water will rise higher in the smaller space and be easier to compare visually. You could also weigh the water if you have a small kitchen gram weight scale.

Results & Conclusion Write down the results of your experiment. Come to a conclusion as to whether or not your hypothesis was correct.

Something more Try this experiment using a variety of different clothing materials: rayon, dacron, wool, fur, nylon, combinations of cotton and polyester.

Project 45

Out of the Middle

Separating liquids by density

Purpose Experimenting with liquids that have different densities.

Overview Liquids may have different "densities." The "density" of a liquid is a measure of how closely packed together its molecules are, which determines its weight and mass. A liquid that is less dense than another liquid will float on top of that liquid.

Have you ever seen chicken cooking in a pot of water to make chicken soup and noticed a layer of fat floating on the top of the water? Some of the chicken fat is separating from it and the fat floats. Since chicken fat is not easy to digest, some cooks pour some or all of this excess fat off before making the rest of the soup.

In whole non-homogenized milk, fat can also be separated by density. This "cream" is less dense than the rest of the milk. Today, machines separate milk and cream, but farmers used to let whole milk stand for several hours so the cream would separate and rise to the top, where it could easily be skimmed off with a spoon.

Hypothesis A liquid can be extracted (removed) from a container that holds one or more other liquids, as long as that liquid has a different density than the other(s).

Procedure Honey is denser than water. Water is denser than vegetable oil. We can use honey, water and vegetable oil to make three separate layers of liquids, all contained in the same jar. The extraction device is CONSTANT. The density of the different liquids is VARIABLE.

In a clear jar (a pickle, relish, or jelly jar will work well), pour in enough honey to make a layer about an inch (2.5 cm) high in the jar.

Fill a drinking glass with water. Add a few drops of food coloring (choose blue, or a color that is different from the honey you are using). Stir with a spoon. This will make the water more visible.

Gently and slowly pour the water into the jar of honey until there is enough water to form a second layer about an inch thick. Next, slowly pour another inch-thick layer, this time of vegetable oil, into the jar. Let the jar sit until the three different layers of liquids are clearly defined.

Let's extract the layer of water, which is in the middle of the liquid layers. To do this, we must construct a device for extracting the liquid.

Seal the top of another clear jar by wrapping several layers of plastic food wrap over it, making a tight seal on the top. Stretch a rubber band around near the top of the jar to hold the plastic wrap tightly in place. Poke two small holes in the plastic wrap with a pencil point, at opposite sides. Insert a foot-long (30 cm) piece of flexible plastic aquarium tubing into each hole. Push one tube into the jar until its end is positioned near the bottom of the jar. Position the end of the other tube near the top of the jar. To make a seal, add a bead of glue around the two holes where the tubing goes through, and set aside to dry. The jar must be airtight.

Take the tube whose end extends near the bottom of the jar and stick it into the other jar containing the three liquids. Position the end of the tube to be toward the bottom of the layer of colored water. Place the end of the other tube in your mouth and suck in on it as you would a straw in a soda to drink it. As you pull the air in the jar out through the tube, the liquid will be pulled out of the jar by the vacuum through the other open tube.

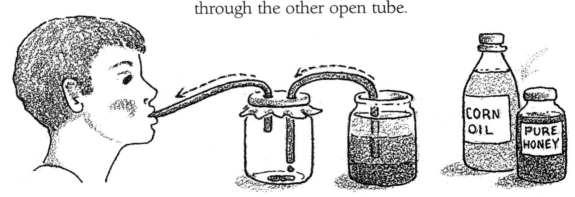

You have successfully extracted the middle layer using the concept of differing densities and vacuum suction—an example of chemistry and physics working together!

Results & Conclusion   Write down the results of your experiment. Come to a conclusion as to whether or not your hypothesis was correct.

Something more
1. Attempt to extract the honey on the bottom of the jar through the vegetable oil.
2. Visit a farm and collect some whole milk in a clear container. Observe the separation of cream over time.

Project 46

Not Just Desserts

Testing taste with combined flavors

Purpose Would combining two different flavors of gelatin dessert create a new flavor, or will the two individual flavors be discernible?

Overview Food companies are constantly trying to improve the taste of their products and also to come up with new products to sell. Recently, a number of these food products have been made up of combinations of flavored ingredients; cranberry-apple or kiwi-strawberry drink, for example.

Gelatin desserts, available in stores as packaged powders that you add hot water to and then place in the refrigerator to gel, are available in many flavors: lemon, lime, strawberry, cherry, raspberry, peach, watermelon, to name a few. If we mix two flavors together in equal portions and make a gelatin dessert, do you think your taste buds will interpret the taste as being a brand-new flavor, or do you think you will be able to detect the two separate flavors?

Hypothesis Hypothesize that when two different flavors of gelatin dessert are combined, a person's taste buds will not be able to identify the two individual flavors. Or, hypothesize that a person's taste buds can identify two separate flavors of gel in a combination. What do you think?

You need
• an adult
• a box of lemon gelatin dessert powder
• a box of lime gelatin dessert powder
• kitchen measuring cup
• spoon
• bowl
• water
• a cooking pot
• use of stove-top burner
• use of refrigerator

Procedure   Read the instruction on the box of gelatin dessert. It will probably say, "Bring one cup of water to a boil. Add the powdered gelatin. Stir until the powder is dissolved. Add one cup of cold water. Stir. Pour into a bowl and let cool in a refrigerator."

Since we are going to use the contents of two gelatin desserts, the quantity of water must be doubled. Therefore, the instructions for making our combination dessert would be: Have an adult help you bring two cups of water to a boil on a stove. Add one package of lemon gelatin dessert and one package of lime gelatin dessert. Stir until the powder is dissolved. Add two cups of cold water. Stir. Pour into a bowl and let cool in a refrigerator.

When the gelatin hardens after several hours, scoop some into a bowl and taste. Does the dessert taste like a new flavor? Can you taste both the lemon and lime? Or does it taste like just one flavor (if so, which flavor dominates)?

Results & Conclusion   Write down the results of your experiment. Come to a conclusion as to whether or not your hypothesis was correct.

Something more

1. Repeat the experiment using different combinations of flavors: Combine lemon and cherry, cherry and raspberry, lime and raspberry and so on. Which combinations of flavor do you like best? Does one flavor usually dominate, or can you tell what two flavors make up the dessert?

2. Compare sugar-free gelatin desserts to sugar gelatin desserts. Hold a box of sugar-free gelatin in one hand and a box of sugar gelatin in the other. Be sure they each will make the same quantity of dessert (that is your CONSTANT; the VARIABLE is the type of gelatin, sugar or sugar-free). Is one lighter than the other? From the nutrition information printed on the boxes, compare the calories of one to the other.

Project 47

Tricking the Brain

When a food's color is changed

Purpose to determine how important color is in our expectations of the taste of a food.

Overview From our life experiences, we learn to expect something that tastes like lemon to be yellow in appearance. We expect something that tastes like cherry to be red in color. Does color really play a big part in how we expect a food to taste?

In this project, a batch of lemon gelatin will be made, with a spoonful given to each of 10 people. Each person will be asked to take a spoonful and try to identify the flavor. The lemon dessert, however, will not be yellow!

Hypothesis Most people will not be able to recognize the true flavor of a gelatin dessert if the natural color of it has been changed.

You need
- an adult
- 1 box of lemon gelatin dessert powder
- red food coloring
- kitchen measuring cup
- 10 plastic disposable spoons
- 10 paper cups
- water
- pencils (or pens)
- 10 small notepad-size sheets of paper
- a cooking pot
- use of stove-top burner
- use of refrigerator

Procedure Following the instructions on a package of lemon-flavored gelatin, ask an adult to help you make a bowl of the dessert. (For safety, it's important that an adult stand by whenever you work around or use a stove.)

Before you place the lemon gelatin liquid in the refrigerator (be careful of splashes), add several drops of red food coloring and stir. Add the food coloring until the lemony-yellow liquid has turned a deep red.

When the disguised lemon gelatin has cooled and hardened, place a spoonful into each of 10 small paper cups. Give 10 people (friends or family members) a cup with a gelatin portion and a spoon. Ask them to each taste the dessert and, without speaking about their choice, to write on a piece of paper the flavor of the gelatin. (Be sure your test subjects aren't being influenced by seeing others' answers.)

Ten people are being asked to give us an idea of how most people will probably answer. Ten is our "sample size." We are using a few people to estimate how many people may respond to the test. A sample size is when a smaller group is being tested which, if large enough, will hopefully give us a true picture of a larger group.

When you have tested 10 people and collected your data, determine the percentage of people who were fooled by the unexpected color. To find percentage, simply divide the number of wrong guesses by 10 and multiply the answer by 100. If, for example, eight people guessed wrong, that would mean 80% of those tested were unable to correctly identify the flavor.

$$8/10 = .8$$
$$.8 \times 100 = 80\%$$

Results & Conclusion   Write down the results of your experiment. Come to a conclusion as to whether or not your hypothesis was correct.

Something more

1. Test the concept of "sample size" by testing 20 people (you only need to ask 10 more people and add those results to the first 10). Compare the percentage of wrong guesses to 20. Is the percentage about the same as it was with only 10 people? Do you think that a sample size of 10 people used in the original experiment was enough to get an accurate result?

2. Are some flavors easier for people to identify, even if the color is different? Try a common flavor, for example orange, and add red food coloring until it is red. Then ask people to identify the flavor. Are more people able to correctly identify orange than lemon, even though both are disguised by a strange coloring?

WORDS TO KNOW

A Glossary

acid is a characteristic describing a chemical substance. Substances that are strongly acidic may "burn" your skin or dissolve other substances. A pickle tastes sour because it is an acid. The opposite of an acid is an alkaline. Chemists use a scale called a pH scale to measure if a substance is an acid, an alkaline, or neutral.

alloy a metal made from a mixture of different metals or a combination of a metal and another substance, which gives the metal new qualities.

apparatus equipment used in a chemist's laboratory; the tools of the trade include flasks, beakers, test tubes for handling small amounts of substances, scales and balances and Bunsen burners.

assumption In doing science experiments, scientists often make assumptions that certain things are true. An assumption is something that is believed to be true.

base substances that are strongly alkaline in the measure of their pH. Alkaline substances may "burn" the skin.

calibrate to make a correction or adjustment to, often to a measuring device. When two thermometers are being used in an experiment, it is important that both thermometers are accurately reporting temperatures. When both thermometers are in the same place, they should both read the same temperature, but if one is higher than the other, it must be noted and the difference in temperature must be added or subtracted from the other one in all experiments where the temperatures on the two thermometers are compared.

calorie For the human body to function, it needs energy. We get energy for our bodies by eating foods. The amount of energy we can get from a particular food is measured in units called calories.

carbon One of the basic elements of matter, carbon combines with many other substances to take on different forms. Carbon can combine with oxygen to form carbon dioxide, a gas that plants absorb to make food for the plant. Carbon is also a residue of burning.

catalyst   something that can speed up, slow down, or cause a change in a chemical reaction. The catalyst substance itself does not change.

caustic   can damage or destroy (corrode or burn) from a chemical reaction.

chemical change   When a chemical change takes place, a new substance with different properties is formed. Rust is produced when oxygen and iron combine. This is different than a physical change, which is when a substance changes from one form to another without a change in its composition; freezing and melting are examples of a physical change.

chemical equation   the use of chemical symbols in formal statement to represent the complex factors that are the result of chemical reaction.

chemical symbols   one or two letter "abbreviations" that represent the elements. Elements are substances that cannot be chemically broken down into simpler basic substances.

colloidal   A colloidal substance is a gelatin-like substance in which the small particles that make it up do not dissolve, but stay suspended in the fluid. The substance may be more like a liquid in one state and more solid like a putty in another state.

compound   A chemical compound is a substance made up of two or more elements in a certain proportion to each other. Compounds often do not have the characteristics of the elements that make them up. Water is a compound containing two parts of hydrogen to one part of oxygen. Oxygen makes fire burn, yet water (H_2O) puts fires out.

conductor   a material, usually metallic, through which electric current flows easily.

crystals   Some substances have a characteristic shape of smooth, flat sides with sharp edges and corners. Table salt and sugar are crystals, with grains shaped like three-dimensional cubes.

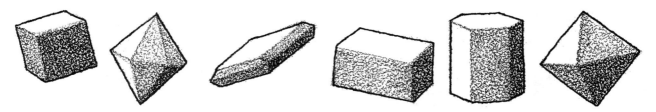

current flow   an energy transfer along a conductor by the movement of electrons.

density   The "density" of a material refers to how closely packed together the matter is that makes up that material. If two objects are exactly the same size, one will weigh more if it is denser than the other one. Objects that are less dense than water will float in it; objects that are denser will sink.

dilute   the addition of liquid to make something thinner or weaker.

dissolve   to break down a substance into a liquid. You can dissolve salt in water.

distillation   a method of extracting or purifying a substance.

distilled water   water totally free of impurities. It can be purchased at supermarkets and pharmacies.

element   a substance that cannot be separated into different substances (except by nuclear disintegration). All matter is made up of elements. There are currently 111 known elements.

endothermic reaction   a chemical change requiring heat for a reaction to take place.

exothermic reaction   a chemical change where heat is given off when the reaction takes place.

fermentation   a chemical change involving the breaking down of a combination of starch and sugar. The combination is turned into alcohol and carbon dioxide gas. When cider ferments, vinegar is formed.

hypothesis   a thoughtful, reasoned guess about something, based on what is known. A hypothesis must be proven by experimentation.

inorganic chemistry   deals with substances that do not contain carbon. Carbon is the chemical of life.

litmus paper   is a device used by chemists to measure the pH of a substance; that is, its acidity or alkalinity. It is a dye made from certain plants. A substance which is an acid will turn blue litmus paper red. Alkalines turn red litmus blue or deep violet. If the solution is neutral, it will not change the color of the paper. Litmus paper is inexpensive to buy. You can make your own by boiling cabbage.

mass   how much "stuff" an object is made of. The more mass it has, the heavier it is. A Ping-Pong ball and a golf ball are about the same size and shape, but a golf ball has more mass.

mixture   When two or more elements or compounds are combined but do not chemically combine to form new substances, the substance is called a mixture. Orange juice, air and sea water are mixtures. The proportions of each element or compound can be in different amounts.

observation   using your senses—smelling, touching, looking, listening and tasting—to study something closely, sometimes over a long period of time.

organic chemistry   deals with all substances that contain carbon; the chemistry of life. The opposite is inorganic chemistry.

oxidation   is a process that occurs when oxygen combines with other substances and changes them. Oxidation can happen quickly as when a log burns in a fireplace, or it can happen slowly as when a metal object oxides and turns to rust. Heat is given off whether the process happens quickly or slowly. When oxidation occurs rapidly, a lot of heat is given off and sometimes light is given off, too.

pH   is a measure of a substance's acidity. On the pH scale, pure water is in the middle of the range, with a pH of 7. A lower number means the substance is an acid. A higher reading means it is an alkali. Litmus paper is a device which turns red when dipped in a substance that is an acid and blue when it is an alkali. pH stands for potential of electricity for positive hydrogen ions.

photosynthesis   the process of a plant making its food by gathering the light energy from the sun. Also needed in the process are carbon dioxide, water, chlorophyll (which gives leaves their green color) and trace amounts of minerals.

quantify   to measure an amount, or "how much" of something

reaction   A chemical reaction is where the bonds that hold atoms together in molecules are broken and rearranged to form different bonds, making new substances. Chemical changes can take place when elements come in contact with each other, when they decompose, or when there is a change in temperature or pressure. Chemical reactions may cause energy to be given off in the form of electricity, light or heat.

residue   solid material remaining or deposited after a liquid containing the material has gone or evaporated.

sample size   a smaller group that takes the place of a much larger group, in order to do a test. The size of the sample group should be big enough to give a true picture of the larger group.

saturated solution   When a substance that is being dissolved in a liquid can no longer be added to the liquid and dissolved, the liquid solution is called a saturated solution. It is easy to tell when a solution has reached saturation, as the substance to be dissolved will start becoming visible in the container, since it can no longer be dissolved in the mixture, no matter how much stirring is done.

solution   a specific type of mixture where the substances are uniformly (evenly) mixed. Sugar in ice tea is an example. The sugar dissolves and is distributed throughout the whole glass of tea. (See mixture.)

solvent a substance that can dissolve another substance, or turn it into yet another substance.

surface tension is when the surface of a liquid acts like it has an elastic skin. At the surface of a liquid in which molecules are close enough together, they attract one another to create a skin-like condition called surface tension. Place a drop of water on a piece of wax paper and it will form a tiny sphere. A pin placed gently on the surface of water in a bowl will float on the water because the surface tension has created a tough "skin." Soap changes the surface tension of water.

tare weight The tare weight is the weight subtracted from a gross weight to allow for the weight of the container. The result gives the weight of the contents of the container or holder. If you want to know how much your cat weighs, but he or she won't sit still on a scale, weigh yourself holding the cat. Then just weigh yourself. Subtract your weight (the "tare" weight) from the weight of both you and the cat and the answer is the weight of the cat.

trace a barely detectable amount of something.

variable something that can be changed.

viscosity the ability of a fluid to flow. A fluid that has a low viscosity flows easily and quickly. Water has a low viscosity; cold molasses has high viscosity.

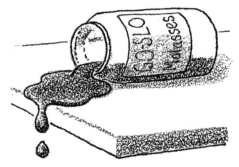

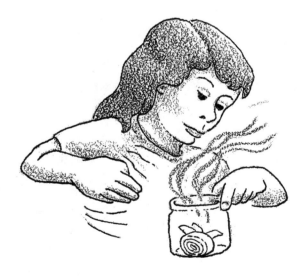

wafting a technique used to safely sample the scent of something without taking a deep breath of it. Holding the object away from your face, wave you hand over it, blowing a few of the vapors toward your nose.

weight the force of gravity pulling on an object downward toward the Earth.

Index

A
acid, 88
concentration by evaporation, 16
dissolution and, 53
litmus testing of, 11–13
reaction with base, 18, 19
artificial flavorings, 8–9
artificial sweetener, vs. natural sugar, 44–45
atoms, 68

B
baking soda
reaction with vinegar, 19
releasing carbon dioxide from, 72–73
base, 88
litmus testing of, 11–13
reaction with acid, 18, 19
battery, 28–29
bread, mold inhibitors for, 20–21
bubble solution, monster, 50–51
burning, 22–23
capturing carbon from, 22–23
as exothermic reaction, 36–37

C
candle power, 37
carbon, 22–23, 88
carbonation in soft drinks, reducing, 26–27

carbon dioxide, 18
for extinguishing flame, 72–73
from fermentation, 48–49
in soft drinks, 26–27
chemical change, 62–63, 89
chemical symbols, 69, 89
chemistry, 5
chlorophyll, 25
"clearing the palate," 75
clothing materials, characteristics of, 80–81
colloidal substances, 7, 89
color
from dye combinations, 58–59
effect on food taste, 86–87
concentration, from evaporation, 16
conductors, 28–29, 89
cooking
effects on pH, 17
of onions, taste change from, 52
copper
as electrical conductor, 28
tarnish remover for, 47
in water, 54
crystals, 78–79, 89
current flow, 28, 89

D
data exactness, repeatable results and, 56–57
density, 89

of liquids, 82–83
of soap, 66–67
digestion, 53
dilution, 30, 90
dissolve, 53, 90
distillation, 55, 90
dyes, natural
combining, 58–59
sunlight and, 38–39

E
eggs, measuring endothermic reactions in, 34–35
elasticity, weathering effect on, 70–71
electricity, conduction of, 28–29
elements, 68–69, 90
emulsifier, 50
emulsion, 40
endothermic reactions, 34–35, 90
evaporation, 16, 80
exothermic reactions, 36–37, 90
extraction, of liquid, 82–83

F
fermentation, 48–49, 90
flavor combinations, taste of, 84–85
food
color, effect on taste, 86–87
dissolving with acid, 53
identification, senses in, 60–61

food additives, for mold inhibition, 20–21
fragrance, releasing with heat, 64–65
fruit, ripening, 42–43

H
heat, releasing fragrance with, 64–65
hypothesis, 6, 90

L
liquids. *See also* water
density of, 82–83
litmus paper, 11–13, 90

M
measurements, accuracy of, 56–57
metal
as electrical conductor, 28–29
oxidation of, 24
milk, sour, 15
minerals, in water, 54–55
mixtures, 19, 90
mold inhibitors, 20–21

N
natural substances, 8–9
nonconductors, 29

O
oil spill, cleanup of, 76–77
onions
taste of, cooking and, 52
vapors from, 46
oxidation, 91
in burning, 22
of metals, 24

P
periodic table, 68–69
pH, 91
cooking effects on, 17

dissolution and, 53
evaporation and, 16
litmus paper testing of, 11–13
pickle taste and, 14
of sour milk, 15
photosynthesis, 25, 91
physical change, vs. chemical change, 62–63
pickling, 14
plants, photosynthesis and, 25
pollution, 30
pressure, physical changes from, 7
protons, 68

R
reactions, 91
acid–base, 18, 19
endothermic, 34–35, 90
exothermic, 36–37, 90
residue, 54, 91
ripening, of fruit, 42–43

S
safety, 5
sample size, 87, 91
science fair projects, 5–6
scientific method, 5–6
smell
in food identification, 60–61
of natural substances, 8–9
process of, 64
releasing fragrance with heat, 64–65
strong substances safely, 10
soap
adding to water, 40–41
changing shape/density of, 66–67
solution, for

monster–bubbles, 50–51
soda drinks, reducing carbonation from, 26–27
sodium bicarbonate, releasing carbon dioxide from, 72–73
solute, 19, 30–31
solution, 19, 91
solvent, 19, 92
spores, 20
starch, in fermentation, 48–49
stomach, 53
sugar
in fermentation, 48–49
natural vs. artificial sweetener, 44–45
ripening process and, 42–43
sweetness of, 74–75
sunlight, natural dyes and, 38–39
surface tension, 50, 92
synthetic fabrics, 80–81

T
tarnish remover, natural, 47
taste
color of food and, 86–87
of flavor combinations, 84–85
in food identification, 60–61
of natural substances, 8–9
sensation of, 74–75
of trace amounts of solute, 30–31
taste buds, 74
temperature, viscosity and, 32
trace, 30, 92

V
vinegar, reaction with baking soda, 19
viscosity, 32–33, 92
volume, 67

W
wafting, 10, 92

water
distilled, 55, 90
extraction of, 82–83
hardness, 51
minerals/residue in, 54–55
oil spill cleanup and, 76–77

physical change of, 62–63
soapy, 40–41
weathering, effects on elasticity, 70–71

Y
yeast, 48–49

About the Authors

Bob Bonnet, who holds a master's degree in environmental education, has been teaching science at the junior high school level for over 25 years. He was a state naturalist at Belleplain State Forest in New Jersey. Mr. Bonnet has organized and judged many science fairs at both the local and regional levels. He has served as the chairman of the science curriculum committee for the Dennis Township School System and is a "Science Teaching Fellow" at Rowan University in New Jersey. Mr. Bonnet is listed in *Who's Who among America's Teachers*.

Dan Keen holds an associate in science degree, having majored in electronic technology. Mr. Keen is the publisher of a county newspaper in southern New Jersey. He was employed in the field of electronics for 23 years and his work included electronic servicing as well as computer consulting and programming. Mr. Keen has written numerous articles for many computer magazines and trade journals since 1979. He is the co-author of several computer programming books. For ten years he taught computer courses for adults in four schools. In 1986 and 1987 he taught computer science at Stockton State College in New Jersey.

Together Mr. Bonnet and Mr. Keen have had many articles and books published on a variety of science topics. They are the authors of the books *Science Fair Projects: Environmental Science*, *Science Fair Projects: Electricity and Electronics*, *Science Fair Projects: Space, Flight and Astronomy*, *Science Fair Projects: Energy* and *Science Fair Projects: Physics*. All are published by Sterling Publishing Company.